Financing women's enterprise

FINANCING WOMEN'S ENTERPRISE

Beyond barriers and bias

Thea Hilhorst
Harry Oppenoorth

Royal Tropical Institute – The Netherlands
Intermediate Technology Publications – UK
UNIFEM - USA

Royal Tropical Institute
Enterprise Development
Mauritskade 63
1092 AD Amsterdam
The Netherlands
Tel. (20) 5688711

IT Publications
103/105 Southampton Row
London WC1B 4HH
UK
Tel. (71) 436 9761

UNIFEM
304 East 45 Street, 6th Fl.
New York, N.Y. 10017
USA
Tel. (212) 906 6400

The Royal Tropical Institute gratefully acknowledges the contributions of

NORAD, the Norwegian Agency for Development Cooperation,
SDC, the Swiss Development Corporation,
DGIS, the Directorate General for International Cooperation in the Netherlands,
and ICEIDA, the Icelandic International Development Agency,

to the symposium *Sharing poverty or creating wealth? Access to credit for women's
enterprises and of* UNIFEM, the United Nations Development Fund for Women,
to the publication of *Financing women's enterprise*

CIP-DATA KONINKLIJKE BIBLIOTHEEK, DEN HAAG

Hilhorst, T.

Financing women's enterprise : beyond barriers and bias /
T. Hilhorst, H. Oppenoorth. - Amsterdam : Royal Tropical Institute
ISBN 90-6832-705-4
NUGI 661/682
Subject headings: women's enterprises ; financing / development cooperation.

© 1992 Royal Tropical Institute - Amsterdam
Editing: Pratt and Boyden Consultants
Cover design: Nel Punt
Printer: ICG Printing

Table of contents

Preface

Women's access to financial services in developing countries was the focus of a symposium organized by the Royal Tropical Institute in Amsterdam, the Netherlands, in January of 1991. Participants from formal financial institutions, women's grassroots organizations, donor agencies and non-governmental organizations discussed the subject in depth (participants and background papers are listed in the appendixes). Among the points of discussion were the role of credit in poverty alleviation, and how to target programmes to women; viable institutional arrangements; the use of subsidies; delivery of credit with or without additional support services; and alternatives to credit. The symposium served as a starting point and stimulus for *Financing women's enterprise: beyond barriers and bias.*

The aim of this book is to identify and analyze the potentials and constraints poor women face in gaining access to financial services; to better understand what is necessary if financial services are to be more accessible to them; to indicate certain needs for future research; and to facilitate improvements in policy and implementation. Programmes are required that meet the demands and needs of poor women, and do so in such a way that services are both financially sustainable and capable of contributing to women's economic and social empowerment.

The underlying assumption – and challenge – has been the idea that bringing experiences, recommendations and theoretical issues related to financial intermediation together with those in 'women's studies' would increase our understanding of the possibilities inherent in designing and implementing financial services. *Financing women's enterprise* is addressed to development programmes or projects, and also to banks of all types, interesting in taking the gender issue seriously, and looking for ways to support poor rural women as they strive to improve their living conditions and obtain an equal position in society. It seems somewhat odd to us that, in these days of million dollar unpaid business loans in Western countries, it should be necessary to justify financial services for poor women – which involve far smaller amounts. Poor women are creditworthy, and given a chance, are good potential clients for financial services.

We would like to thank the United Nations Development Fund for Women for their financial support of this publication. It is our hope that the information presented will not only contribute to the ongoing debate, but also will help to encourage taking the financial demands and needs of poor women seriously. In the long term we hope this will help rural women in developing countries to improve their living conditions and their social position.

Vera Gianotten
Head of the Enterprise Development Programme,
Royal Tropical Institute

Acknowledgements

This book is the product of a shared experience in which many persons and organizations took part. First of all, participants in the symposium on women's access to financial services, organized by the International Forum of the Royal Tropical Institute (KIT), brought their expertise into the discussion.

Vera Gianotten, John Grierson and Ton de Wit provided the original idea for following up the symposium with a book; without their enthusiasm and constructive criticism this publication would perhaps not have been completed. Many people have directly or indirectly contributed. To list them all would be impossible, but we wish to acknowledge in particular conversations with Frits Bouman, Margarita Guzmán, Martin de Jong, Aart van der Laar, Sarah Mangali, Klaas Molenaar and Frits Wils. Others, who read early versions and made extensive and valuable criticisms, include Susanne Engelhardt, Bram Huisman and Lida Zuidberg. Finally we thank KIT Press for a last round of editing.

Having said all this, Jo Boyden and Brian Pratt – who did substantial editing of our final draft – must be mentioned. They really did the impossible; they translated our strange sort of language into English, and restructured some parts of the book. Their efforts have made publication possible.

While those mentioned do not bear the responsibility for the end result, we very much appreciate the support they gave as we worked to relate the many issues explored here to our experiences in development cooperation.

Thea Hilhorst
Harry Oppenoorth

Introduction

Women's enterprise takes myriad forms, and so do their needs for credit. Access to financial services can be needed simply to help an income generating activity continue, but, if applied well, also can sometimes serve as a catalyst, facilitating working conditions and allowing an increase in the income generated. While this is true for the economic activities of both women and men, women's needs for finance, the impact financial programmes have for them, and their rationale in seeking and using finance may differ. Further, to an even greater extent, existing financial systems, including those established by development projects, often set barriers – among them, stereotypes about women and economic activities that lead to bias in granting credit – that obstruct women's access.

Financing women's enterprise: beyond barriers and bias looks specifically at women and their need for finance, ways this demand is met at present, and how access to adequate financing and financial services can be enhanced. 'Finance' generally refers to credit and savings, but occasionally includes other forms of financing, such as risk and profit sharing. The aim is to combine the information available from the many experiences of financial programmes, with the accumulated insights from both women in development (WID) programmes and gender studies. Beginning to bring together the two worlds of finance and gender may eventually provide a way to improve programmes intended to better women's access to financing.

The emphasis in this book is on access to financial services for poor, self-employed women. The relatively small group of 'less poor' female entrepreneurs, involved more or less full-time in their enterprises, certainly face gender biases and gender-specific constraints. However, financial intermediation to serve them is less complicated, and ways have been found – if not always put into practice – to adapt financing to their specific needs. Special attention is given to rural areas; the focus in past discussions of need for financing has often been on urban women.

Considering finance and gender side by side points up a number of factors. Poor women are generally involved in a variety of low-return activities, in which the combination of gender inequalities and poverty increases the adversity of working conditions. The search for ways to earn a livelihood becomes even more critical in times of economic recession. This is especially true for women, since the number of households they head – in which women and children can rely only on their own capacity to generate an income – is rapidly increasing.

For these women, as for those who are not heads of households but whose families need extra income, the only option is often to generate their own income, via self-employment, despite the problems they face in gaining access to assets and resources. Opportunities and possibilities open to women are more limited than those for men, and freqently must be compatible with other obligations. Gender roles (that is, the culturally determined roles of women and men) affect the division of labour, as well as access to and control over the allocation of resources and benefits. Self-employed women, and even more so women employed in family-based labour, may have little control over allocation of their earnings or products: women are often subordinate, with limited control over their economic lives. Not only living conditions but also womens' position in the household and society, and the accompanying social change required for sustainability, are at issue: this has essential implications for the design of programmes offering financial services.

The access of most poor women to formal finance is very limited indeed. In addition to stereotypes that have generally prevented banks from seeing women, and particularly poor rural women, as prospective clients, their lack of collateral, the small amounts often needed and inappropriate delivery systems (among other factors discussed in later chapters) make the use of formal financial services difficult. Programmes established in relation to development programmes have also not always been well suited to such women's needs, or have not been sustainable. Thus far, women have had to rely primarily on informal sources of finance, which also have a number of disadvantages but are relatively accessible.

Financial interventions have the potential for making major improvements in the lives of poor women – when they take poor women's enterprise and gender-specific conditions as a starting point. The very good repayment records of women who have participated in financing programmes have demonstrated their creditworthiness, and it is to be hoped that their value as clients will come to be recognized. However, finance is not automatically appropriate in every situation. Enterprises run by women also operate under many non-financial constraints; whether financing for these concerns (and even more for family-based activities) will have a positive impact for women in a particular situation must be carefully evaluated. The macroeconomic context and policy environment within which women's work occurs can also limit the impact of enhanced access to finance.

Combining insights

In recent decades, a wide range of projects and programmes involving women have been implemented; many studies have also been done on rural women's work and gender position, and the impact of development programmes in these areas. A great deal of experience has been accumulated, and theories have been developed to explain gender inequalities and subordination. Unfortunately, most of the resulting experience and insights are not common knowledge outside specialist circles.

Until recently – and still to some extent – the work and needs of women have remained almost invisible in most development strategies for rural areas. Most assistance (credit, technical assistance, training) has been directed to men, or male dominated activities (Deere, 1984; Palmer, 1985). Where the income generating activities of women have not been ignored, they have often been seen, implicity or explicitly, as having only marginal importance.

Development models have assumed that benefits accruing to men would automatically benefit women and other household members. Experience has shown this is frequently not the case. In addition, it has been taken for granted that women would work within development projects, benefiting the household or the community while being excluded from all decision making and management responsibility. Not only did women receive no direct support (and few indirect benefits); often interventions contributed to deterioration in their living conditions and increased their work load. Further, the changes in access to resources resulting from development interventions have often been detrimental to women and their enterprises (Whitehead, 1985; Lycklama à Nijeholt, 1987; Young, 1988; Kandiyoti, 1990).

Normative, and often western, ideas on how men and women should behave have been projected onto development programmes. Stereotypes have dominated views of the division of labour. It has been assumed that women were or should be confined to the domestic sphere, and were not or should not engage in market oriented production. Often, however, discrimination has been more subtle. Rules governing cooperatives, credit, training and land reforms have been written in ways that in practice left women out. Thus gender biases have excluded women from many development programmes.

Negative experiences with development programmes led to the implementation of programmes and policies that target women explicitly. Most such projects, however, focused initially on women as (incapable) mothers, teaching them how to clean and feed their children and take care of their homes. Income generation later became an issue, but even then development work has tended to focus on projects that make use of women's assumed 'domestic' skills, rather than beginning from women's existing enterprise, and seeking out and teaching skills for which there is a market. Unfortunately such projects, based on assumptions about women's roles and abilities, became the model for supporting rural women. They are remarkably uniform in both tone and content, despite their lack of success (Kandiyoti, 1990; see also Chapter 5).

A major problem with the use of such traditional models is that within existing social institutions women are generally subordinate to men, so that they often have no control over the products of their labour and thus benefit very little from the resulting programmes. Programmes have nevertheless declared themselves in favour of integrating women into overall development. This suggests a misperception, since women are in fact integrated into society – though not always into development programmes. The failure lies with the programmes, not the women. (Lycklama à Nijeholt, 1987.)

Designing appropriate programmes for women is, however, not necessarily easy. Among the difficulties is the diversity of their roles, activities and situations. The socio-economic roles of women involve both productive and reproductive work (which includes domestic work and caring for other household members) in the household and community, and are of a seldom-appreciated complexity. Their economic activities must not conflict with their other roles. Moreover, there is no single category 'women'. Within any region their situation varies with class and social stratification. There are opposed interests among women of distinct strata, and programme impact on income will vary among various categories of women (Young, 1988; Kandiyoti, 1990).

Financial interventions

Although programmes for women have been few in number, three decades of more generally targeted credit programmes and the efforts of development banks have produced valuable lessons. More recently, new approaches have been developed by the 'peoples' banks'. The results of these experiences have been widely debated; opinions on the various approaches and institutional arrangements differ widely (e.g. Donald, 1976; Howell, 1980; von Pischke et al., 1981; Adams et al., 1984; Devereux et al., 1987; Maloney and Ahmed, 1988; Bouman, 1990; Floro and Yotopoulos, 1991). Among the issues in question are the importance of credit to development; the neglect of savings and self-finance; the role of informal sector credit; the merits of parallel schemes versus mainstream formal financial systems; reducing transaction costs; the use of subsidies; financial sustainability of institutions; tied credit; targeting; the type of activities to be assisted; how credit should be delivered; what the conditions and support services should be, and how to pay for these.

Women's access to these financial programmes has only recently entered the discussion. Some programmes have adapted their approaches to facilitate access. Various case studies of the participation of women in financial programmes have appeared (e.g. DeLancey, 1978; Chen, 1989; Berger and Buvinic, 1989; Buvinic and Berger, 1990; Noponen, 1990). Analyses of gender-specific aspects of financial intermediation are beginning to become available (these include Berger, 1989; NIO, 1989; Holt and Ribe, 1990; Slob, 1991).

In analysing gender-specific aspects of financial intermediation, this book attempts to begin to bridge the gap between theory and development practice. It is hoped this will aid in the design of programmes that are effective and truly relevant to large numbers of poor rural women. Integrating the experience of the two fields of knowledge implies addressing not only improvements in women's production and income, but also women's position in relation to men.

Plan of the book

Before increasing financial services to women, it is necessary to ask whether, in the situation at hand, credit is indeed an instrument that can lead to economic development; and, if so, what the impact of macroeconomic policy conditions will be. On one hand, this is the question of the role of supply-leading versus demand-following finance; on the other hand, it relates to the question of appropriateness of finance for those modes of production that do not (or scarcely) involve market oriented production and trade. Where credit is appropriate, from these points of view, is examined in Chapter 1. The history of credit interventions in development efforts is then briefly reviewed, especially with respect to assumptions about scarcity of capital, and to targeting credit (including tied credit) and subsidizing interest rates. This provides lessons that can be applied in considering credit delivery for poor women.

Chapter 2 treats women's work and needs for income. The impact of differences in the social roles of women and men (gender roles) are covered briefly here, and further in Appendix 1. Women's work consists of activities in the productive and reproductive spheres and includes community obligations. Women's involvement in productive activities is discussed, both within the household production unit and in women-managed activities. The critical issues of women's decision making and control over income are also raised. A short description of the characteristics and dynamics of women-managed enterprises concludes this chapter.

The various roles and situations of women, and the many activities they perform, produce a wide variety of financial needs. Each activity includes a sequence of production process elements, any of which might be improved with finance. The importance of savings to economic development for poor women is covered, and their role in decision making, often greatly affected by the part they play in production, is further explored in Chapter 3. This provides the background for a discussion of the possibilities, problems and consequences of various types of financing – working capital, credit for productivity improvement or for marketing and trade, and finance for productive group or community activities. The issue of targeting financial services to particular categories of women is covered, as is the need for flexibility in financing.

Chapter 4 turns to the question of informal finance, including self-finance. Women's needs for financing are already being met, to some extent, often by this means: informal finance is present everywhere. Women make extensive use of various informal sources, and participate in many self-help savings and credit organizations. Informal finance definitely responds to needs. It is often reasonably adequate, but also has limitations, including gender bias. The characteristics which make informal finance attractive to poor women are explored in Chapter 4, as are the limitations. Sources, including savings, relatives and friends; rotating savings and credit associations (Rosca's); and moneylenders, pawnbrokers, and merchants are detailed. Among the issues of interest is whether some of the approaches used here might also be applicable within the formal financial system.

Finance is, however, not only supplied by the informal sector or by banks. Many development projects include a credit fund, and there has been a great deal of practical experience with revolving and rotating funds. Furthermore, savings and credit cooperatives have been formed in many countries. In some countries, peoples' banks have been established during the last decade, and have been an obvious success. Therefore the solutions such projects, funds and organizations apply to problems encountered in providing banking services to the poor are of interest. Their experiences, and especially those of institutions that target women, will be examined in Chapter 5.

At present, poor rural women and often women in general have little access to formal finance. Even where formal finance is in principle accessible, the use women make of this source remains limited. Thus it is important in the short term to develop specific programmes for women. Nevertheless, it is to be hoped that mainstream financing for women's enterprises will someday be a normal expectation, rather than an exception. And in fact, if large numbers of women are to be served by financing, with continuity built in, increasing women's access to the formal financial sector must be a long term goal. This sector and its constraints and opportunities with respect to meeting poor women's financial needs are therefore discussed in Chapter 6.

The Epilogue highlights the need for more information on the effectiveness of financial interventions for poor women. Programmes will, however, continue to be designed in the interim. Thus certain key issues in planning interventions, including the role of the development programme with respect to finance, the need for local information, and the need to build evaluation of effectiveness into programmes, are briefly explored.

Chapter 1

Credit interventions: context and history

Awareness of the importance of women and their enterprise[1] to economic development has only grown in recent years; availability of credit for poor women is now a concern. However, attention to credit – without a focus on women – has had, within both aid agencies and governments, a much longer history: it has been seen as crucial to the development of farms and other micro-enterprises in the Third World. Thus in considering credit programmes for women, it is well to look at the experience of earlier programmes in similar settings. First, however, Chapter 1 will examine some of the factors determining the impact of credit on the development of small enterprises, and especially those run by women. These include the external constraints associated with the macroeconomy and the legal and political environments that affect credit for micro-enterprises. Poor households may follow an extremely wide range of production strategies, but all are affected by the general economic, political and legal conditions in society, and ultimately these latter may be more decisive than local factors when it comes to the success or failure of the enterprise.

Macroeconomy and policy environment

Enhanced access to credit may, under favourable conditions, result in an increase in production. However, if there is no effective demand for the new products or services, income will clearly not expand. On the contrary, an increase in production at a time when demand is low can lead to greater competition and reduced prices, thereby undermining rather than increasing incomes.

In open economies, demand depends on both export and national markets. And as far as the latter is concerned, there may be wide disparities in demand in rural and urban areas. The proportions of the export, urban and rural markets not only vary from country to country, but may also change significantly over time. In general, though, it can be stated that more than half of the production of both non-agricultural and agricultural goods in rural areas is consumed within the rural sector itself (Kilby and Liedholm, 1986).

Small enterprises are subject to numerous forces which are effectively beyond their control. For example, demand in rural areas is determined by a series of factors extraneous to the product itself. It is determined in part by the level and distribution of income, which, in turn, is closely related to the prices of agricultural products and the distribution of land. Demand is also determined by cultural preference and by the value attached to imported or urban produced substitutes as compared to local produce. Thus, as preferences change, handmade goods often give way to mass-produced items, and eating habits may change; in many countries, imported white flour has replaced locally grown staples.

Demand for rural products in urban areas is also subject to cultural preference. But factors such as infrastructure and marketing channels, income distribution and competition with urban or imported products are equally as crucial. Thus, under conditions of widespread poverty, unequal income distribution, low levels of social services and poorly developed infrastructure, demand is not likely to expand rapidly (UNDP et al., 1988).

Government policy can play a major role in determining the state of the national economy and shaping the market. In many developing countries, for example, agricultural food prices are kept artificially low as a subsidy to urban populations. The abolition of price controls on food generally has a favourable impact on rural incomes, and thus on demand for other production from rural areas. Although urban consumption is initially reduced by higher agricultural prices, this effect is not normally long term – particularly in the case of staple products with inelastic demand.

Demand can be further stimulated by policies which reduce income inequality, in that a small increase in the income of large numbers of poor people will expand the demand for basic goods and services. The concentration of income in the hands of a few, on the other hand, tends to stimulate demand only for small quantities of luxury, mainly imported, goods.

The impact of interventions such as credit and training, which are designed to increase supply, will be limited when demand is poor. In such circumstances, income may be redistributed without a net increase in overall production. The encouragement of the production of goods in carefully selected areas where existing production does not meet demand may be an exception. Otherwise, it will be necessary to introduce policies that stimulate demand before significant changes in the incomes of the poor can take place.

In recent years there has been a tension between economic policies designed to increase demand economically, and structural adjustment policies, which have a deflationary effect. The exact conditions of adjustment policies vary between countries, but the general aims are the reduction of public expenditure,[2] privatization of state enterprises and banks, liberalization of markets, export promotion and local currency devaluation. The result is often that the economy is stabilized, at the cost of reduced production, income, and consumption, and of higher unemployment (Meilink, 1991). While under these circumstances new income and employment opportunities are needed, this may be difficult to achieve at a time when demand is drastically reduced.

Although structural adjustment policies are said to be gender neutral, the evidence is that in practice women are affected differently, and more severely, than men (Commonwealth Expert Group, 1989; Elson, 1989; UNICEF, 1987). Women who manage household budgets will be the first to experience the impact of rising prices for basic goods and services.

During the 1960s and 1970s the urban and rural poor were commonly thought to be underemployed (Elkan, 1973; Little et al., 1987). It was assumed that in time industrial investment would absorb the underemployed, increase incomes and reduce poverty. Thus, the argument was that credit and savings had to be mobilized for investment in the industrial sector, and that credit for micro-enterprises would not benefit the national economy since it would merely reinforce low levels of productivity.

That small enterprises may make more efficient use of capital and labour, and that their contribution to the economy is far greater than was earlier imagined, is now widely recognized. More recently, the important role of women in small scale enterprises has been acknowledged (Liedholm and Mead, 1986; ORU, 1988; Haggblade et al., 1989; UNDP, 1988). However, there is still much to be learnt about the role of small enterprises in the national economy, and there is a need to review the conventional approach of neoclassical development economics in this light. For example, it is not clear to what degree the expansion of small enterprises merely replaces the production of middle-sized concerns, rather than increasing the total circulation of goods and services in the economy. It is evident, however, that under certain circumstances credit can greatly assist small enterprises with the expansion of output, turnover and incomes, reflecting both a latent demand for their goods and a capital shortage at the micro-level for meeting these demands. When the supply of capital presents a more serious obstacle than does demand, those few people who have access to it can make relatively high profits by meeting local demand, which would otherwise be frustrated by the lack of supply.

In some situations (for instance in isolated poor rural areas), though, demand is simply too small to maintain production and services for local use alone, and transport costs are too high to justify bringing these goods to the cities. Many of these limitations are, however, not insurmountable, in that they are local rather than national. For example, in Sudan small business schemes flourished in a number of urban and semi-urban communities when rural demand was at an all time low due to severe famine (Pratt et al., 1988).

It has already been suggested that non-economic constraints such as unfavourable government policies and politically determined distortions in the market can have a serious effect on micro-enterprises. Thus, restrictions on small enterprises due to inflexible legislation can have a severe impact. Studies of Lima, Peru, have shown that the legal procedures for registering small enterprises are extremely time consuming and expensive, an impossible burden for most businesses (de Soto, 1986). As a result, many enterprises are not registered and large numbers of people are obliged to work outside the law.

Women in business face many additional, gender-specific obstacles. For example, legal frameworks still assume that men are invariably the heads of household, the prime property-owners and major decision makers. In many countries women require the signature of a husband or male relative to open a bank account, obtain loans, or enter into business contracts. Even when laws are changed in favour of women, it is still common for banks and other institutions to insist on rules that treat their female clients merely as appendages of male relatives. There is a great deal of scope for radical change in national legislation, by-laws, business and banking codes and procedures, to permit the development of small enterprises.

Experience with rural credit schemes

Many attempts have been made to expand the volume of agricultural loans. Special credit lines have been created and in some cases financial institutions have been established for this purpose. After two decades of experience with rural credit provision it is now possible to make a fairly comprehensive analysis of its strengths and weaknesses. While expectations of the potential impact of credit were high at the outset, in many instances performance has been disappointing. It is worth reviewing this performance – especially in relation to women's enterprises – to highlight some of the problems and limitations of credit. Three aspects will be considered: first, the need to determine whether an increase in supply of funds will actually be beneficial; second, targeting of funds; and third, subsidized interest rates for end-users.

Increasing supply of funds
Lack of capital has often been considered the most important single constraint preventing people and businesses from taking advantage of profitable investment opportunities. It is argued that if credit were available on proper terms, both diversification and expansion of production would be more feasible. Capital scarcity, it is suggested, is caused by the limited overall availability of formal credit, access to which is particularly problematic for small-scale enterprises. Informal financial services, such as those of moneylenders, have been judged as too expensive and exploitative to provide an acceptable alternative to formal provision.

Poor access to formal credit is thus considered a crucial obstacle to development. It is also a problem policymakers believe they can resolve in the short term. Because credit in the main entails channelling money, it is an instrument favoured by donors who may hold large amounts of funds that they are anxious to disburse. Furthermore, finance for credit programmes is perceived as being relatively easy to direct and administer (de Jong and Kleiterp, 1991; Meyer, 1989).[3]

Some of these traditional assumptions need to be challenged. It is important to investigate, for example, whether in a given situation scarcity of capital is the real bottleneck, and whether new financial interventions are necessary to stimulate development. While an objective of many early credit programmes directed to small-scale enterprises was an increase in the overall amount of loanable funds within the formal financial system, it is not clear there was in all cases a shortage of capital. It has also been argued that in many areas such interventions are redundant, because provision of financial services automatically follows demand, and existing formal (commercial) banks and informal financial services together cover the need (Bouman, 1989).

In many countries, however, financial institutions are not geared to credit provision for small businesses, but mobilize capital either for large conglomerates, or for the public sector deficit. Elsewhere, the legal framework makes it virtually impossible for commercial financial institutions to operate to the benefit of the small enterprise. Some governments have tried to force banks to provide services to poor people by establishing a system of quotas, under which a set proportion of lending must be targeted at a specific group. However, obligatory quotas are difficult to enforce and easy to evade:

special credit lines have remained marginal, and reporting requirements designed to ensure compliance have merely increased transaction costs, making the loans even less attractive to banks. The quota system does not therefore hold much promise as a way of increasing the access of poor women to the formal financial sector (Levitsky, 1989; McKee, 1989).

Targeting credit
Two types of targeting are common to rural credit schemes. The first entails directing credit and related services to specific types of production, or specific sectors of the economy, with the aim of encouraging production of certain goods or crops. The second aims to benefit certain types of enterprise, or certain specific socioeconomic groups. Thus, some programmes have tried to channel services to medium-scale or 'successful' enterprises, while others have seen poverty alleviation, or the meeting of gender-specific goals, as their priority.

Sectoral targeting has commonly been associated with what some have called the 'small farmer approach'. Credit has been tied to the purchase of predetermined inputs, such as new seed varieties or fertilizer, intended to increase production in sectors of the economy selected as priorities by government and aid agencies. In this approach credit use is normally restricted to specific crops or activities. Often, specialized financial institutions, such as agricultural development banks and agricultural programmes, are established to operate alongside pre-existing services. Under sectoral targeting, credit is the only financial service offered. Other services, such as saving facilities and money transfers, are not made available (World Bank, 1974; Meyer, 1989).

In the sectoral model, planners and policymakers have generally ignored the fungibility of money,[4] and assumed that it is possible to channel credit to specified activities that they consider the most productive and beneficial for development purposes. In this context, credit has been viewed as an input, similar to seed or fertilizer, with a direct causal effect on production. This perception has resulted in expectations regarding the potential impact of credit on agricultural output that are in practice unrealistic. Complicated mechanisms, requiring considerable and costly administration and control, have been developed to direct loan use. But in spite of these attempts to channel credit, borrowers tend to find ways of utilizing the funds to suit their own needs; numerous evaluations note such diversions of loans (Adams, 1988). This is entirely rational, from the borrower's point of view. But where loans are used for consumption, there are no sales to provide cash to repay loans.

The rather disappointing results of the sectoral model are mainly the result of misconceptions regarding both the informal and formal financial sectors and the financial demands of the target group. Planners have failed to assess real financial needs, as well as the role and function of informal financial institutions (Morss, 1976). In light of the very 'top-down' nature of sectoral targeting, perhaps we should not be surprised by its failings. The financial institutions created under such schemes have seldom proved viable and self-sustainable, and have not been shown to serve small farmers on a long term basis (Meyer and Nagarajan, 1988). In introducing small-scale credit for women, it is important to take the failings of sectoral provisions into account, and to avoid making the same mistakes.

The second approach to directing credit entails social targeting, or giving priority to especially poor or powerless groups of people, rather than focusing on the economic sector in which they work. Various methods are possible. A decision may be taken, for example, to direct credit to activities that have low levels of productivity but provide widespread employment for a target group. Alternatively, entrepreneurs in those sectors or branches that allow for capital accumulation and increased value added may be supported in the hope that by doing so the poor will obtain employment and gain in the long run.

Since credit is a scarce resource, it is important when taking decisions about targeting to be clear which socioeconomic groups will benefit and why. For example, the second option implies that the poor – and especially poor women – will not themselves receive direct support. Further, while it is tempting to support larger, more successful, enterprises with potential for growth – on the assumption this will have greater impact on national economic development – the formal sector has proved largely incapable of absorbing the labour force and maintaining the population economically. This has been true in particular during times of recession. The newly-industrialized Asian countries, such as Singapore and Taiwan, are among the rare exceptions to this general rule.

There is a growing realization that the informal sector has been far more efficient than once thought in absorbing the unemployed and providing the means for economic survival of a large proportion of the population in many countries. It is likely that because of the lower capital cost per job created, the cost of providing employment and a livelihood in the informal sector is far lower than in the formal. In addition, labour and capital mobility is higher in the informal sector than in formal industrial concerns, or in the public sector or parastatals. Therefore, in times of rapid economic change – whether positive or negative – smaller enterprises are better able to adjust than larger, more bureaucratic concerns. Indeed, in recent years these latter have become a drain on most national economies, rather than an asset.

In light of these factors, and given the limited resources available to improve income and employment, it is probably more effective to lend small amounts to people engaged in labour-intensive activities than to lend to larger formal concerns. There are indications that small-scale credit, provided in a flexible and adapted way, allows many small enterprises to stabilise their production and provide an income for considerable proportions of the population who would otherwise have no means of survival. Given that many poor women are found in this segment of the economy, they are apt to benefit as well.

On the other hand, the effect on the target group and the community must also be considered. For example, an economy with a low degree of market incorporation may be severely impacted by the introduction of credit. The introduction of credit alone can create conditions that lead to restructuring of production. Work directed at sales to external markets may increase, and with this comes increased dependence on external inputs. The degree of differentiation and polarization in the community may increase. Credit provided for working capital may favour those with greater access to fixed capital (including land or water), as opposed to those with few resources at their disposal. Thus it is important to assess the possible impact of introducing credit into such an economy.

Subsidized interest rates for end-users ('cheap credit')
Another assumption, common in early micro-credit programmes, was that small-scale farmers and entrepreneurs were too poor to pay interest at market rates or to generate appreciable savings. Furthermore, it was argued that subsidized interest rates could increase income and capital accumulation for specific target groups, thereby changing overall income distribution. Differential interest rates were thus introduced, with the lowest rates being allocated to the priority sector and ceilings sometimes being established for the agricultural sector as a whole. By offering financial institutions discounts on loanable funds, or by directly subsidizing interest, governments and donors maintained interest rates at artificially low levels.

However, these cheap funds often failed to reach the intended target group and, using their influence, more powerful groups secured access to this source for themselves. It is now argued that market interest rates have to be charged precisely to reduce the attractiveness of loans and stop wealthier groups monopolizing cheap credit (Holt and Ribe, 1990; Buvinic and Berger, 1990). Even when intensive supervision and control ensure that at least a portion of the target group is reached, other problems are common. The artificially low cost of capital results in over-optimistic expectations concerning the viability of enterprises, and subsidies have often proved difficult to phase out. Also, this approach has served to promote capital-intensive, at the expense of labour-intensive, production, by artificially reducing the cost of capital as compared to labour. This entails a high social cost (Harriss, 1987).

Subsidized credit can of course be profitable for those borrowers lucky enough to obtain access; the more so if – as has often occurred – repayment can be avoided. Many such programmes have been politically inspired, with either debt cancellation in the run-up to elections, or borrowers who felt no obligation to repay. Since banks do not always take action, default has proved a major problem in these programmes and loan delinquency has been the rule. In this way, funds have gradually been depleted.

Due to the low interest ceilings and the large numbers of small loans development banks have been expected to disburse, these programmes have not been able to cover their transaction costs. The low level of profitability from such transactions has discouraged savings because local depositors cannot be attracted. Financial institutions have thus become completely dependent on external funding and more vulnerable to the policy changes of government and donors. This has threatened the sustainability of financial institutions and severely restricted access for subsequent borrowers (Levitsky, 1989; Meyer and Nagarajan, 1988).

Subsidized interest rates for end-users have thus been discredited, and are widely criticized because of their destructive impact on the financial system (von Pischke et al., 1981; Adams, 1986; Holt and Ribe, 1990). It is unfortunate that so much damage has been caused by these schemes and banks have come to accept, unjustifiably, that loans to small businesses are unprofitable. It is possible that certain very disadvantaged groups will not be able to initiate income generating activities without subsidies, legitimating the use of cheap capital. However, even in these cases, it is preferable to combine grants and 'normal' credit rather than subsidize interest rates (Harper and Momm, 1988).

Summary

a) Small enterprise development in rural and urban areas is strongly influenced by external factors, and especially by the economic and political environment and the legal framework. Some of these forces are susceptible to lobbying (for example legal rules on banking for women), while others (such as market prices) are not so readily changed for the benefit of the small enterprise.

b) When there are severe constraints on the macroeconomy, it is not always clear how far the level of production of goods and services can be increased. It is argued that in such situations, even the most successful of small-scale credit programmes can only hope to redistribute income and markets to the benefit of the poor, rather than expanding markets overall.

c) There is a need to review earlier experiences with credit programmes before initiating new interventions targeting women. It is important to learn from the problems of the past in such areas as tied credit, subsidized interest rates, high transaction costs, political interference and the lack of sustainability of many institutional models of delivery.

d) It should not be assumed that credit is the only, or even the major, constraint to the evolution of small enterprises run by women. It is essential that a full needs assessment be carried out to specify the exact problems faced by these enterprises in a given situation, and what alternative solutions, including credit, might exist.

Notes

1. Unless otherwise stated, 'enterprise' refers to urban and rural, agricultural and non-agricultural, formal and informal, businesses of all sizes.

2. In agriculture, health and education but never in military budgets (Hancock, 1989).

3. In some institutions this analysis has changed. In many countries, sufficient funds are now considered to be available to banks in the local formal sector for short term lending. However, a relative scarcity of funds for long term loans persists, due to the high proportion of short term deposits (de Jong and Kleiterp, 1991).

4. Fungibility refers to the fact that funds, once received, may be used for any purpose.

Chapter 2

Women's work and income

The economic crisis of the 1980s intensified poverty throughout the world; among the effects have been changes in the economic roles of women and men. While unemployment and the cost of living have both increased, the returns for many products have been reduced, thereby eroding incomes. Men, women and children are all under pressure to make up this shortfall. In female-headed households, women, together with their children, are the main providers of household income. Further, it is estimated that on average more than a quarter of households in Third World countries are headed by women. Although considerable regional variation exists, globally the number of de facto female-headed households is increasing (Moser, 1989). Female-headed households tend to be among the poorest (Clark, 1984; Whitehead, 1985).

This chapter first explores the impact of social differences between women and men on production and on the control women have over resources within the household. Women's responsibility for reproductive work, including childcare and housekeeping is discussed, and the implications of such obligations for the generation of income are highlighted. A discussion on the importance of self-employment is followed by a summary of some characteristics of women's enterprises, with a short exploration of their dynamics and development patterns. Local conditions, the socioeconomic characteristics of the household, and individual abilities will all affect opportunities for self-employment, as will norms and values with respect to ways men and women should behave and ways resources and labour should be divided between them.

Household based production

A household is usually defined as a residential unit whose members share consumption and production. Functions and boundaries vary among societies and over time (Brydon and Chant, 1989). The needs, rights and responsibilities of members of a household are sometimes sharply differentiated on the grounds of gender, age and other factors.[1] The distribution of resources and income among household members may be far from equal. Thus, while household members sometimes in part have common goals, they do not necessarily have the same economic interests. Because the interests of various members of a household may differ radically, it is now widely accepted that intrahousehold relations must be taken into account in the planning of development measures. It cannot be assumed that women or children will automatically benefit from interventions directed at the household in general.

Economic production within a household may have a collective base. In addition, individual household members may obtain their own income from wage labour or self-employment. There are many different ways in which income from collective and individual activities are distributed or shared. In some societies all income is pooled, whereas elsewhere it is both held independently and shared. There are also households, especially in parts of West Africa, in which male and female income and assets are kept completely separate (Cloud, 1985; Baud, 1989; Standing, 1991).

When women work in family-based enterprises, not only their tasks but also their influence is determined by local custom, including gender roles for their age group and position in the family. This includes specification of their bargaining power. An important factor is the extent to which they are involved in decision making, including decisions concerning the allocation and control of benefits. Unfortunately, their participation in decision making is often weak and their work undervalued. Even when women contribute significantly to the household income, their participation in decision making may remain minimal, as for example is the case with female carpet weavers in rural Turkey (Berik, 1987). Working in family-based enterprises can also limit the time available to women for more profitable self-employment.

Because there is so much variation in these areas, development agencies should make a location specific analysis of existing household production systems before planning interventions. This should include a gender-based analysis of the production system. Such an analysis will identify who performs what tasks, decision making processes, and the allocation of returns from the perspective of individual members. This will highlight and make more explicit the various gender roles (for a possible methodology, see Overholt et al., 1985). Such an analysis will also make the different sources of income and the importance of family-based production in meeting basic consumption needs evident. Questions such as whether financial interventions are needed and whether they will also benefit women who work as family labourers (for example by strengthening their influence on decision making) need to be confronted.

Control over income

Income is clearly not the only factor that determines the socioeconomic position of women. It does appear, however, that the overall status, bargaining position and income of women who are wage earners, self-employed traders, artisans or farmers is higher than that of women who are confined to domestic or subsistence activities (Brydon and Chant, 1989). But even when women bear the costs and risks of setting up an enterprise, they may not control the benefits. Thus it is not enough to increase the capacity of women to generate income; they must also be able to control their returns and to protect their sources of income and assets.

In West Java, as one example, it has been noted that 'if women's enterprises grow in scale and capitalization, quite commonly husbands – who previously played only a minor, if any role in the enterprise – insert themselves as managers, the women then regressing to the status of unpaid family member' (White, 1991, p. 22). Also, when a certain activity becomes profitable, even when previously considered as women's work, men seek to become involved, bypassing the traditional division of labour and possibly even accepting the lesser status of the work. This process is commonly observed when labour-saving technologies are introduced (e.g. Whitehead, 1985). It is clear that poor women need support to maintain their position in successful income-generating activities.

Another problem is that men may reduce their contribution to the household budget when it becomes clear that a woman's income has increased. This not only restricts the capacity of the woman to save and invest in her enterprise, but also leaves her with the sole responsibility of maintaining her dependents. When the man's contribution to the household decreases, women need assistance to ensure that their husbands become more 'integrated' into household production and family life (Stølen, 1991).

An effect of an increase in income for women can be that men feel threatened by a loss of status. Alternatively, they may fear that their partners will leave them once they have secured their independent source of income. Husbands may start to obstruct their partner's enterprise if the earnings become greater than their own. There are also examples where men have reacted with violence to changes in a woman's economic status, as when women have sought to reduce their unpaid obligations to men in favour of their own work (Bruce, 1989; Gianotten et al., 1990). Development programmes cannot ignore the problem of such violence.

Reproductive work

One crucial difference between the role of women and that of men is the way in which, almost worldwide, women are held responsible for reproductive activities. In this there is close complementarity in the labour of women and children, with mothers sharing tasks with their older offspring. A fall in household income can result in an increase in the burden of reproductive work, as women are obliged to reduce the use of commercial services and products that save labour. Furthermore, in many countries public services are becoming more costly, forcing women to seek additional funds. Quite apart from the direct drain on household budget, a reduction in efficiency of essential services increases the reproductive labour burden. Thus, for example, women may spend a great deal of time waiting in queues to take advantage of health services.

Time-allocation studies reveal that women normally work longer days than men, especially when reproductive activities are taken into account. They are often the first to rise in the morning to light the stove and prepare a meal. And when others have retired at night, they continue to work, cleaning the kitchen, preparing food for the following day and so on (Dixon-Mueller, 1985; Grown and Sebstad, 1989). Reproductive work is usually not remunerated because neither men nor women perceive it as real work. Nor is the time invested in such activities taken into account or costed. These oversights contribute powerfully to the undervaluing of the economic role of women at both national and local levels.

The labour productivity of reproductive work is generally low, due to the absence of, or limited access to, labour-saving technologies and services. In rural areas, basic services such as piped water, grinding mills and shops may be lacking, increasing the burden of housework. Commonly, women find that one of the costs of stepping up their business is a proportional increase in their working day, because their other responsibilities remain equal.

Women's domestic obligations influence their scope for engaging in economic activities; many women are forced to engage simultaneously in more than one activity. For example, they may care for their children while also working in the fields or selling products in the market. Furthermore, they may have to interrupt their work regularly in order to attend to children or prepare and deliver food to their husband. These multiple demands on their time restrict women to sectors of the economy where flexibility is possible. Thus the time and energy spent by women in reproductive labour limits the time allocated to earning an income. It also restricts the mobility of women, explaining in part why they lack access to channels of information and have only limited experience of dealing with public (including financial) institutions.

Women are therefore generally more concerned than men with issues such as health, food security, and labour-saving technologies for use in reproductive work. Access to credit for reproductive activities such as grinding mills and other labour-saving devices may be as important for women as access related to income generation. If credit results in a reduction of the time consumed by non-income generating activities, it may permit devoting more time to earning income.

The importance of self-employment

An increasingly large proportion of women are self-employed, often in the 'informal' sector. They engage in an almost limitless variety of activities. This trend is largely due to the shortage of formal employment for women, pressure on rural economies and rapid urbanization in many parts of the world. It is important to note that involvement in the informal sector also has some advantages for women – therefore this trend should not be regarded as purely negative.

Wage work in the formal sector is often more stable and better rewarded than in the informal, but women are at a particular disadvantage when it comes to competition for formal employment.[2] They often lack the education, training, and experience required, for example, and may not have the contacts needed to secure work. Even when women have the expertise required, in almost all countries and sectors there is marked discrimination against them; women are overwhelmingly present in less prestigious and lower paid occupations. Even if men and women undertake the same type of work, women do not always receive the same wages and benefits as men. It can also be culturally unacceptable for women to enter certain work sites or certain occupations; or their mobility may be restricted. They may be excluded from the more public social spheres, including formal employment. (Dulansey and Austin, 1985; Lyberaki and Smith, 1990).

Further, formal employment can entail disadvantages for many women. The rigid work routines common in most formal concerns, together with the travel to and from the workplace, may be difficult to combine with domestic duties. Self-employment, on the other hand, allows more flexibility in both the work schedule and the place of work.

Home-based production, in particular, can be easily combined with reproductive work.

Working in the informal sector does, however, present some difficulties. Working conditions can be harsh. Since entry is relatively easy, competition can be fierce, and this reduces earnings. Moreover, wage labourers in the informal sector are not protected by laws concerning contracts, wages, social security or health and safety regulations (Levitsky, 1989). Finally, labour relations such as sub-contracting or piecework can result in extreme dependency on one or more firms or intermediaries for credit, equipment, raw materials or marketing outlets. In such cases, the extent to which self-employed women are able to make their own management decisions is limited. (White, 1991; Baud, 1989).

Despite these disadvantages, self-employment is an important source of livelihood for women in developing countries. According to labour statistics, more than half of the economically active women in Sub-Saharan Africa and southern Asia are self-employed and in northern Africa, the rest of Asia and Latin America, the figure is around one-third (UN, 1991).

Women generally engage in self-employment as part of a household production system. In female-headed households especially this may constitute the main source of income. Alternatively, women may balance participation in household based enterprises, wage work, self-employment, and reproductive work. The particular combination of activities in which women are involved will have implications for their selection of economic strategies and activities. Women may, for example, select activities that generate continuous earnings to make up for the seasonal nature of men's farm income, even though these activities may not be the most profitable. It has also been observed that women's involvement in activities that are low risk, although often low return, act to guarantee basic consumption, allowing other household members to invest in ventures that are more risky but have greater potential for profit (Downing, 1991; Grown and Sebstad, 1989).

Employment of women by sector
Throughout the world, many rural women work in agriculture. According to labour statistics, one-fourth to one-third of these women are self-employed, while the others work as family labourers or wage workers (UN, 1991). In some regions a process of feminization of agriculture is occurring, with women managing farms while their husbands migrate elsewhere in search of employment.

Despite the importance of women in agriculture, their access to land is still restricted. The size and quality of landholdings are less for women than men and since few hold titles of any sort, their tenure is generally insecure. This reduces women's capacity to invest in production or expand agricultural activities. Moreover, access to credit – whether for agricultural or other purposes, and whether from institutional or informal sources – can depend on having a clear title to land as a guarantee of collateral. Under these conditions, many rural women are forced to explore alternative activities to increase their incomes.

In rural areas, significant numbers of self-employed women are involved in manufacturing and services, mainly in small or micro-enterprises. More women seem to own or manage enterprises in these sectors in rural than in urban areas (UNDP et al., 1988). For example, women account for a substantial proportion of both management and employment in non-farm enterprises in rural Africa (Haggblade et al., 1989). However, it should be noted that the percentage of women varies greatly by sector and scale of enterprise (Downing, 1991).

The significance of off-farm production in rural areas may be influenced by settlement pattern, among other factors. Thus, non-agricultural activities are more important in rural towns than in more dispersed villages. The productivity and extent of growth in the agricultural sector are also causal: because it operates within a network of consumption and production linkages, agriculture can generate sizable employment and income multipliers in the rural non-farm economy. (Haggblade et al., 1989; UNDP, 1988).

Rural populations often combine work in agricultural and non-agricultural sectors. It is estimated that about half of rural women engaged in agriculture also obtain some income from non-agricultural activities. Households with small landholdings generally obtain a greater portion of their income from non-farm sources than those with large holdings. This is in part a sign of distress and adaptation to increasing levels of unemployment, poverty and landlessness, and may act as a buffer when earnings from agriculture are poor (UNDP, 1988; Haan, 1991; Pye, 1988). However, certain individuals or households may specialize in craft production, and some may work exclusively as traders or shopkeepers.

As rural areas develop, non-agricultural activities are likely to gain in importance in relation to agricultural. The impact on rural women's income and employment will vary from one sector to another. For example, in the manufacturing sector, a shift away from more traditional production is to be expected, and products like baskets and pottery may be replaced by plastic utensils. Women often dominate the more traditional sectors. Thus, in this process of transformation they will tend to lose employment and income (Liedholm, 1990). On the other hand, commerce and services – sectors in which women are often predominant – become more important (Haggblade et al., 1989).

Characteristics of women's enterprises

Self-employed women face the multitude of problems common to all small-scale entrepreneurs. These include limited access to capital, inputs and markets. Often a large number of small enterprises share one market segment, causing competition to be fierce and prices low. The products of small enterprises must also compete with those of larger concerns and with imported items. Small enterprises can be extremely dependent on a limited number of suppliers and wholesalers. This renders the entrepreneur economically vulnerable and often exposes her or him to exploitation (Tovo, 1991; ORU, 1988; Levitsky, 1989).

Gender inequalities, however, are such that businesses headed by women are consistently worse off than others. Women generally have fewer resources than men, and are impeded by lower levels of education and literacy, and by restricted physical and occupational mobility. They find only very restricted access to more profitable activities, and their skills are often common to large numbers of other women, so that work in these areas is generally highly competitive, oversubscribed and poorly paid. Too, women have fewer contacts and less bureaucratic know-how and bargaining power than men, which still further limits their productivity and profitability. Legislation often favours men against women in the distribution of land, inheritance and divorce settlements. Business associations and service agencies designed to support small enterprises may be mainly directed to men, limiting women's access to their services (van der Wees and Romijn, 1987).

Intra-household conditions concerning the division of labour, decision making, and control over resources and output provide a second group of constraints. Women have less control over their own labour than men, because their productive work competes with reproductive roles and obligations. They find it difficult to secure access to resources, as well as control over the allocation of their returns. Confidentiality about a woman's possessions and income can be essential if she is to avoid losing control of them to other household members (Okelo, 1991).

Enterprises run by women tend to be small even by the standards of the informal sector. They are usually run on a part-time basis to allow women to meet their other obligations. Generally extra labour is not contracted, although the enterprise may depend heavily on the unpaid labour of children (Holt and Ribe, 1990; Dulansey and Austin; 1984).

Poor rural women are involved in a variety of productive activities, as determined by both local and personal opportunities and constraints. Their enterprise is often composed of a range of different activities, in combinations that may vary over time. Rural women may be engaged in agriculture during periods of peak activity in the crop cycle, and in off-farm wage labour at other times of the year. Involvement in a diversity of tasks makes it very difficult for women to develop specialized occupational skills. Indeed, it has been argued that 'specialization is a luxury only the better-off can afford' (Epstein, 1990, p. 254). There are of course exceptions: some women do possess large areas of land, manage major enterprises, or become dominant traders in a profitable market niche.

Dynamics and development patterns of women's enterprises

The dynamics and continuity of women's enterprises are often influenced by household composition and the life cycle, which in turn determine labour availability, financial and kinship obligations and household needs. The presence of child labour, for example, is crucial in terms of the potential to increase household income (Bequele and Boyden, 1988).

Economic factors, as suggested by the preceding section, also play a role. Some women do secure funds for investment, but this is generally harder for women than for men. On the other hand, a lack of capital is not the only factor that may impede growth: women are more likely to work in low-return sectors than men, so their profits are lower; women often spend a relatively high proportion of their profit on household needs, and generally have less access than men to use of household funds for investment (Bruce, 1989; Grown and Sebstad, 1989; Carr, 1990).

In addition, while expansion is generally seen as a way of gaining from economies of scale, it is also apt to increase risk. It is only possible to take risks where there is a secure source of income, such as from wage employment, ensuring that basic consumption needs can be met (Downing, 1991). Further, increasing activities beyond a certain scale will require major adaptations in the way a small enterprise is organized. The enterprise is likely to become more formalized, the division of labour more complex, and management skills more crucial. Work also becomes more demanding and less compatible with women's other obligations and activities. Too, larger enterprises are more visible than smaller ones, and may have to be legally registered. With registration, the enterprise becomes subject to various regulations and taxes. Many entrepreneurs decide not to expand simply to avoid these problems (Lyberaki and Smyth, 1990). For all of these reasons, the opportunities created by enlarging an enterprise may be more interesting to men than to women.

Thus, the apparent absence of dramatically high rates of growth in individual enterprises should not be taken to indicate failure. Indeed, it is questionable whether most poor women who participate in such ways have as an objective a major expansion in their business. Research indicates that poor women prefer to expand only to the limits of their own labour and management capabilities, assuming that their basic consumption needs have already been met (McKee, 1989).

Most female entrepreneurs appear to select a lateral growth pattern, increasing the number, rather than the size, of the enterprises in which they are engaged (Tinker, cited by Downing, 1991).[3] Some women invest in concerns run by their sisters, brothers, mothers or other members of the family, thereby increasing the security offered by the kinship network (Downing, 1991). Thus, the growth and dynamics of women's enterprises cannot be measured simply in terms of change of scale, or of the profitability of a single firm. More attention to the qualitative aspects of growth, the risks involved, and the influence of gender, is needed. (Lyberaki and Smith, 1991; Downing, 1991).

Summary

a) Women and men within the same household have different prospects in life. Gender roles – modified by other socioeconomic variables – affect who controls the allocation of resources and benefits, as well as the division of labour. To consolidate any economic gains, financial interventions have to be selected according to their potential for making improvements in the position of women with respect to decision making.

b) Since so many women work in household based production, it is particularly important that financial interventions in this area are preceded by location-specific analysis, taking gender into account.

c) It is essential that women be able to control their returns and protect their sources of income. This too will require local information and care in design, so that programmes provide support.

d) Women's self-managed enterprises and activities are conditioned by what is considered normal in a given culture and at the household level, and must be compatible with other activities and objectives. In addition to these issues, poor women face the multitude of problems confronted by all poor people and small entrepreneurs. In light of this double set of constraints, their enterprises tend to be smaller than men's and concentrated in the least profitable sectors of the economy.

Notes

1. Gender, which is culturally determined, is discussed further in Appendix 1.

2. There are exceptions. Certain labour intensive industrial branches such as textiles, shoes and electronics have been reallocated to developing countries. These large-scale plants employ primarily young women, who are paid less than adult men would be. This enables employers to maintain a competitive edge by reducing labour costs.

3. It has been suggested that growth by multiplication of the number of firms, rather than increasing their size, is not gender specific, but a more general strategy common to the informal sector, especially in Africa (Liedholm, 1990; Haan, 1990).

Chapter 3

Women and finance

Supply of credit, as discussed in Chapter 1, is regarded by many planners and policy-makers as the cornerstone of development: it ensures the success of income and employment-generating activities and of schemes to introduce new technologies. Credit has become a common feature in programmes promoting business opportunities for women and, although capital shortage is not the only difficulty faced by small enterprises, it is undoubtedly important and deserving of considerable attention.

A principal constraint faced by poor women in their attempts to improve their living standards is simply lack of income. Credit can act as a catalyst in expanding both enterprises and income. However, in most cases, economic development for women is not obstructed by financial factors alone: quite apart from institutional antipathy, a lack of access to resources, raw materials, new technologies, markets, knowledge and training are all serious problems for women. If a credit programme is to be successful, therefore, additional services may be required to help women to overcome these barriers.

Many of these problems are, moreover, interlinked. For example, low demand commonly forces women to provide additional services, such as selling on credit, to obtain customers. This frequently results in serious liquidity problems, especially when customers are slow to pay off their debts. The women themselves may not perceive the situation this way, believing the lack of finance to be the main constraint. Women whose supply of key inputs is insecure may compensate by holding too much stock, and this not only depletes working capital, but also fails to solve the underlying problem. It is clear that need for credit must be placed in the economic context of other potential threats to the success of small enterprises, as well as of possible solutions.

This chapter thus suggests that women require savings and credit facilities to meet a multitude of different needs, which must be seen in the context of their economic activity. It is argued that, above all, flexibility in savings and credit provision is essential if the economic needs of women are to be given priority.

Savings

The role of credit in economic development is often emphasized, but the importance of savings underestimated. Savings are as crucial to the macroeconomy as to the micro-business and the individual. They serve to mobilize capital for the functioning of the financial system, and provide security for the individual and family. They also permit the rapid expansion of a business to meet new opportunities, act as evidence of the financial probity of the saver and provide funds for personal use, thereby protecting businesses from decapitalization.

In spite of their poverty, a large proportion of women on low incomes save. This allows them to balance the household budget, pay for major purchases and meet emergency needs. They may also require savings to pay for seasonal and special ritual events such as weddings or religious festivals. Clearly, however, the capacity to save will depend on levels of both income and expenditure.

Women without independent incomes generally find ways of saving from the household budget and using methods that guarantee control over their savings. Thus, they may save in goods rather than cash, for example, and hoard them secretly, or place them with others. If women have access to funds of their own, derived from work, inheritance or a gift, these can be converted into jewels, animals, or stocks of products known to be in demand locally. Money and valuables can also be put in the custody of female relatives, friends, the moneylender or pawnbroker; or the woman may participate in a rotating savings and credit association (Rosca).

When there is a risk of losing control of savings to other members of the household, women generally strive to keep their financial status secret. Hiding money can be risky, and stories of theft or of notes being consumed by insects are common. Money placed in the custody of moneylenders or pawnbrokers is better protected and more secure. Also, it serves to establish creditworthiness for future loans.

There are some advantages to holding funds in kind rather than in cash. Such savings are a sort of protection against inflation, and are also more accessible. But again, saving in kind is not without risk: loss and robbery can be a problem; livestock may die; other items can deteriorate or lose value. Moreover, even though goods saved in kind may increase in value due to changes in the market or, in the case of livestock, may reproduce, there is no assurance of interest. In addition, saving in kind may cause liquidity problems. On the other hand, in times of inflation or conflict shedding liquidity may be a major objective of holding savings in kind (Bouman, 1989).

Given the importance of savings to many poor women, it is crucial to protect their value by securing a rate of interest above that of inflation. In some societies women convert savings into credit by obtaining the latter either against the value of their own savings or, via membership of credit and savings groups, from their peers. (See, for example, the section on Rosca's and credit unions). Savings deposits are also important to the sustainability of the financial system. For example, in many countries mechanisms such as post office savings schemes are used by the public sector to mobilize capital for development.

Unfortunately there has been little attempt to disaggregate information on women's saving according to income and occupational sector or sub-sector, their place in the life cycle, or the use to which savings are put. This lack of detailed information makes it more difficult to determine how external interventions aimed at reinforcing savings may best be used to benefit women.

Decision making and place in production

Women are likely to be able to take best advantage of available credit if they can control its use. Therefore, financial intervention must be adapted to the position women occupy in the production process. A distinction has to be made between situations in which women manage an entire enterprise or activity and those in which they work, but are not involved in management. Credit programmes for businesses run by women will not benefit other categories of women, such as those who work as unpaid family labour or employees, but who are excluded from decisions concerning production and investment.

Credit for household production units and enterprises
Determining how and by whom decisions are made in household enterprises can be very difficult, not least because the perceptions of men and women differ and are internalized as part of the ideology of gender roles. This means that in granting credit, the impact for women is not always clear.[1] It could be argued that since in household enterprises the various members of the household work together, credit should be given to the group as a whole through the household head. Many programmes follow this option. The problem is that by adopting this method, funds are almost invariably chanelled through the senior male in the household; in practice, women may receive little benefit. Indeed, the position of women is sometimes undermined by such schemes, isolating them further from economic decisions and adding to their workload without increasing their incomes.

Many poor women spend much time in household production units, assisting their husbands. Financial interventions that strengthen the decision making position of women in this situation should be encouraged. Where credit is offered explicitly to women, it should support their participation in production and give them exposure to financial institutions and procedures. In this way, programmes offering credit to women can make a considerable impact on their status and bring their economic role within the household to the fore (Oppenoorth, 1990).

Another approach is to insist that women be co-signators to loans awarded to household enterprises, are included in any services connected to the loan (such as training programmes), and are party to all information available on financial matters. However, it must be recognized that although women may appear to be fully involved in such schemes, it may be that in practice the impact on their lives is minimal. Thus, for example, men could use women's signatures to endorse their application for funds and share liability for the loan, while in fact allowing them no power in the enterprise. To achieve a real increase in the rights and responsibilities of women is a long process, and one that requires continuous monitoring and adaption. Alternative approaches have to be explored in the provision of loans for household production units, and the feasibility and impact of offering credit only to women, rather than to both men and women, continuously reassessed.

Women-managed activities and self-employment
Women who are in charge of an enterprise, an economic activity, a crop or field, who manage the production process without major interference from others, may assume complete control of credit and benefit from it directly. The situation is more complex, however, for those who control only a part of the enterprise. Their relationship with other members of the household needs to be analyzed and specified before development interventions are attempted.

Enterprises managed by women generally differ in a number of ways from those run by men. Financial services and systems of delivery should cater to the specific needs of women. For example, credit should be sufficiently flexible to allow for the fact that many women engage simultaneously in a series of different activities. Targeted credit made available for a specific sector, a certain crop, or product, is of little benefit to the many women who do not specialize in their work.

Credit schemes should also take into account the specific constraints faced by women. Since they frequently have little to offer as collateral, they require either unsecured loans, or loans based on non-traditional collateral arrangements. (See Chapter 6.) Poor women have particular need of small, short-term loans. This is because in general their turnover is low, their capital revolves fairly quickly and they lack the confidence to contract larger loans. It is important to provide these facilities with the minimum of delay, to allow clients to take advantage of economic opportunities as they arise. It is also helpful if serial loans can be made available, because this facility will permit women to slowly increase loans and capital stock as the business develops and their managerial capacity improves.

Possibilities, problems and consequences of finance

Working capital
The provision of working capital is essential if poor women are to overcome the cash flow problems that so often destabilize their enterprises. Working capital will be required to cover both subsistence (or labour) costs and the costs of raw materials and stock prior to sale of the resulting goods and/or services. Many women engaged in lengthy production processes, in which returns are delayed, borrow in order to meet the cost of their own labour, as required to meet the daily consumption needs of the household. Credit may also be necessary for the bulk purchase of raw materials and other stock, enabling significant discounts to be obtained and reducing the costs of production and sales. In some cases, growth can best be achieved by providing credit to women to enable them to hire labourers. This can be especially effective where cultural constraints inhibit women from undertaking certain tasks in the production cycle.

Credit need not be confined to cash production, since it can also be used to improve subsistence. For example, women involved in subsistence production may need credit to purchase seed and other such inputs. Since the product is not to be sold, repayment has to be made from the returns of other household activities. Of course, these latter activities may well be managed by men. The means of repayment must be made clear from the outset and, to ensure a firm commitment to repayment, all parties concerned – men and women – should sign for the loan.

Informal sector sources of credit, such as moneylenders and local shop keepers, are crucial to the provision of working capital in many communities. However, in some cases this form of credit may be extremely expensive. Substituting can be very helpful to women's enterprises and at the same time reduce their dependency.

Credit for improving productivity
The provision of credit is often combined with the introduction of new technologies intended to increase productivity and income, but which also increase risk. In agriculture, improved technology generally increases the level of specialization, in terms of both the division of labour and the range of products. Specialization increases the vulnerability of the small farm to variations in production due to climatic change or disease, or to a decline in terms of trade. Mixed farming has the advantage of spreading risk among a range of different crops and livestock. An increased return from capital investment cannot necessarily be guaranteed, and profit may be subject to wide local variations, making the indiscriminate introduction of new technologies paid for by credit a hazard for the farmer.

In farming, women face risks over and above those they experience in other enterprises. New techniques and seed varieties are often poorly adapted to the crops women cultivate. They are also often disadvantaged in other ways, in that their land may be of poorer quality than men's, or less accessible. Here too, women are constrained by the multiple calls on their labour.

The introduction of machinery in non-agricultural activities should increase per capita output and reduce the labour burden. However, capital investment may have an adverse effect, and demand for labour may be reduced to such a degree that it results in unemployment. The use of new technologies may well have gender-specific consequences, effecting changes in the division of labour, decision making, and control over traditionally female activities, as well as those jointly implemented with men. When the introduction of such technologies entails a shift from subsistence to market production, or a change in the scale of production, women are often replaced by men, or become less involved in decision making. It is especially common for men to dominate production processes when they become mechanized. This explains in part why most new jobs in the artisanal sector are occupied by men (Pye et al., 1988). Assuming that a new technology is appropriate to the needs of women, priority should be given to making it directly available to them. Many women have been the victims of poor market research and product testing by agencies introducing new ideas and technologies. Care must also be taken to carry out feasibility studies, ensuring that the possibility of failure due to inadequate preparation is reduced to a minimum.

All investment and economic activities, however, carry a degree of risk. The problem with making credit available is that producers may not be able to repay loans, and consequently lose their assets and become indebted. In addition to the immediate problems for the debtor, this can endanger their long-term credit status, disqualifying them from future loans, and undermining their self-confidence. Thus, the introduction of new technologies should be accompanied by risk-sharing forms of credit provision, subsidies or an insurance against risk (see Chapter 6).

Credit for marketing and trade
The provision of credit for marketing and trade is vital, because these activities are central to the livelihoods of so many women. Indeed, the greater part of untied credit presently available for micro-enterprises, whether run by men or women, is absorbed by trading rather than manufacturing enterprises.

There is, however, some debate as to the value of supporting trade-based enterprises rather than manufacture. For example, it has been argued that the latter has greater impact on employment and income (Gamser and Almond, 1989). Others, however, identify trade-based services as key growth sectors in rural development (Haggblade et al., 1989). On the other hand, distinctions among sectors are not always precise. Thus, a large number of small-scale trading enterprises also produce the goods they sell, such as cooked and processed foods or handicrafts. Such an element of manufacturing is seen in many petty trading activities. It could be said that to restrict financial support to manufacturing means imposing an additional barrier to the economic participation of women, given their predominance in trading activities (Buvinic and Berger, 1990).

Before encouraging the expansion of petty service activities, it is very important to ensure there is sufficient demand. In economies experiencing limited growth and a low level of demand, competition becomes so fierce that returns from many activities will be minimal.

Where women dominate the processing of agricultural goods produced by men, an approach to credit which prioritizes the sector can benefit both men and women by improving the vertical integration of the local economy. With credit, moreover, small producers can often avoid being forced to sell in non-competitive markets, to sole buyers, or when prices are at their lowest. Also, prices to producers can be greatly improved when credit is accompanied by supportive action by grass roots producers' organizations, such as bulk storage of products.

Credit to improve productivity of domestic work
A particular need for women is to have access to technologies that reduce the labour time absorbed by reproductive activities (including work such as grinding grain, fetching water, cooking and washing clothes). By cutting back on the demands of domestic work, women gain more time for income generation and leisure. However, the adoption of domestic technologies appropriate for women, or the introduction of innovations in other areas of women's work, is constrained by factors such as access to capital and the degree to which the economic interests of husbands and wives coincide (Whitehead, 1985).

Commercial services aimed at reducing the time absorbed by domestic tasks are increasingly available in urban areas. Rural communities, on the other hand, tend to be poorly served in this regard, because profit is curtailed by low demand and high cost.

Investment to relieve the domestic burden in rural settings, therefore, deserves special attention. Since this kind of investment frequently exceeds the financial capacity of individual women, collective commitment may be required. The provision of piped water to reduce the time absorbed in water collection, for example, must at the very least involve the community as a whole, and may even need investment by government.

If loans are to be made to meet reproductive needs, it is important to establish how repayments will be made. As suggested, expenditure on domestic technology does not normally generate a return to be used for loan repayment. It is possible, though, to calculate the time liberated by the loan, which can then be diverted to income generation. It is also worth investigating the overlap between the domestic or reproductive spheres and the productive. For example, a house might not only provide shelter for the household but also a place of work. This means a loan to improve the roof, in addition to keeping the family warm and dry, will protect the stock of the household enterprise. Further, given that many expenditures in the domestic sphere concern the family as a whole, there is no reason why women should take sole responsibility for repayment, even though the loans may be most directly related to their work.

Finance for productive group or community activities
Small-scale agricultural production is generally carried out by the household unit, according to a more or less rigid division of labour between its members. Other types of production also rely heavily upon different combinations of household labour. Rarely is production for private or household consumption carried out at the community level or by producers' groups, despite the existence of joint or reciprocal labour exchange relations in many areas. Exceptions can be found in some tribal or other traditional societies.

Important economic relationships do, though, exist at the community level in a large number of countries. Many activities undertaken at this level are geared to improving the production of individual households. For instance, communal labour is frequently used to improve irrigation facilities for farmers, or to introduce or expand community services such as schools or drinking water. Some communities possess communal resources such as land, water or forests, which are allocated to member households and exploited at that level. Where they are responsible for livestock, women may have specific interests in improving certain communal services, such as cattle dips.

Projects that finance communal activities should take into account how they affect women since, especially in the absence of formal ownership or usufruct rights, it is possible for women to lose control over and access to communal resources.

Experience shows that programmes intended to introduce communal systems of production are unlikely to succeed in areas where such systems are not customary: they may serve experimental or training purposes by demonstrating a new approach to a group, but not much more. Unfortunately, it is widely believed that community or joint production is 'better' than individual and, moreover, that it is especially appropriate for women. But the history of enforced collective enterprises is not very positive. There are many problems with the approach, including the lack of continuous participation, private appropriation, lack of real economic gain for members, and deficient management (see Chapter 5).

Scope for joint activities does, however, exist when groups of women share common interests and a desire to work together. Often schemes such as these do not embrace the whole community. The potential for collective action is greatest when services are required that no single individual can afford, and demand is sufficient to justify the expense. Group finance may assist the joint purchase of inputs or raw materials, and can help to support joint storage, transport and marketing operations. Bulk purchase can facilitate considerable discounts and free women from exploitative contractual arrangements. Group finance can also be used for buying machinery where the individual economy would not justify such an investment. In this case, an organizational framework must be developed if joint management is to be introduced, as detailed arrangements have to be made about the maintenance, use and future replacement of the machinery.

Targeted credit for poor women

To ensure that women benefit from credit, and to counteract past biases against them by financing agencies, it is advisable to directly target women in service provision. As shown in Chapter 1, the most common forms of targeting rely on distinctions made by sector (for example, agriculture), activity (baking, for instance), or socioeconomic status (such as caste, ethnic group, or all those earning less than an agreed sum). In the case of women who are involved in a series of activities rather than being specialized, targeting by sector or activity can be difficult. Before implementing targeted programmes, though, it is important to establish that the services offered actually meet the needs and demands of poor women. Furthermore, any gender-specific barriers and constraints to credit should be identified and removed.

Schemes offering subsidized credit to specific socioeconomic groups have proved problematic, in that they tend to attract women and men from outside the target group. It is often almost impossible to ensure that the subsidized credit reaches its intended beneficiaries. The leakage of financial assistance from targeted groups is less likely when credit is offered at market prices.

The misdirection of preferential services can also be reduced by involving the target group itself, or intermediary organizations with good contacts with the group, in the selection of beneficiaries. Financial services can be tailored to the specific needs of the target group, thereby making the scheme less attractive to others. Many agencies have found that offering only relatively small loans and insisting on group guarantees discourages richer women from trying to access preferential services targeted to the poor.

The long term goal of targeted programmes should be to become superfluous. To make targeting unnecessary requires an improvement in the outreach of formal financial institutions and improved access of women to formal market credit. Reduction of transaction costs and risks is equally important to encourage more institutions to lend to poor women. Loan conditions should also be as flexible as possible to allow individuals to obtain the exact service they require.[2]

Women do not constitute a homogenous group. Particularly disadvantaged or needy sectors must be identified for targeted credit. Clear, simple criteria are required to define the intended beneficiaries. It is possible that those included in such schemes will become more affluent than those excluded because the latter fail to meet the membership criteria. It is important to avoid penalizing people who are excluded and causing resentment, to the detriment of the programme. Similarly, when preferential conditions are offered it is important to establish an effective system of control to avoid domination of the programme by non-target groups. To stop the development of rules that are excessively complex and reduce the cost of control systems, the definition of categories should be flexible (Batley and Devas, 1988).

Flexibility in financing
It should be clearly understood that there are many situations in which credit services for women are highly appropriate. It is a mistake to place artificial constraints on financing; an open mind and flexibility are needed if credit is to meet its full potential for women. No activity should automatically be disqualified for financial support. While reasoned judgement is clearly required to assess the effect of the loan and the capacity for repayment, and normal commercial practice should always be observed in such assessments, credit for poor women should above all respond to their perceived needs, and not the preconceptions of planners or bankers. Often both credit agencies and women themselves are handicapped by their lack of vision in terms of what is acceptable as a basis for contracting a loan.

When flexibility is exercised in the administration of credit it will permit female clients to identify and state their most pressing capital needs, whether for direct productive investment, repayment of earlier loans, or expenditure for consumption. The provision of dispassionate and professional advice on the use of credit can also help ensure that strategies are adopted that avoid risk. A flexible approach also gives clients an incentive to be open about their perceived needs and the opportunities they identify as most promising, which helps to deal with the fact that finance is fungible.

Summary

a) While capital shortage is not the only difficulty faced by women, it is undoubtedly important. Credit interventions for women should aim to improve production and income, and introduce labour-saving technologies. Programmes that make credit available should also be aware of effects on women's status and visibility, and specifically the influence on the extent of their decision making role.
b) Savings are an important source of investment capital. Women save in money and kind, and use services available in the informal sector. They need to be able to take advantage of secure and accessible savings facilities, which may also facilitate their use of credit. Confidentiality in matters to do with savings is important, especially when women have little control over their income.
c) When women are involved in a family based enterprise in a male-headed household, finance should preferably be offered to men and women jointly. Women who manage

farms or enterprises should be given direct access to credit, through gender-specific delivery systems.

d) It has been argued that women need credit for many purposes, including working capital to cover inputs and labour costs, investment in productive technology, trade and marketing, time-saving devices and services to reduce the burden of reproductive tasks, and perhaps for some group activities. Virtually every imaginable activity, situation or element in the production cycle may prove apt for support through credit; therefore no sector should be excluded a priori.

e) Targeting may help women secure access to finance, although it is necessary to use techniques to reduce the misdirection of preferential services to more affluent groups.

Notes

1. Often, while men produce, women are responsible for processing. If the entire production process is carried out within the same household, the distinction between women who provide family labour and activities managed by women can be unclear. For example, if women process oilpalm fruits, which are harvested by their male partners from their own palms, the work may be perceived as part of the household obligation. If women buy oilpalm fruits from their partners, possibly even on credit, the result is a woman-managed activity. The essential difference is not in the work undertaken, but the structure of decision making and control over production and processing. If men's production and women's processing take place in separate households, women are likely to have more control over the output.

2. However, unlike maturities, repayment schedules and collateral arrangements, interest rates cannot easily be made flexible.

Chapter 4

Informal finance

Most poor women rely on informal financial sources. While these sources can be effective, it is important to note that the informal financial system does not function independently of the gender biases of the wider society. In areas where there are serious constraints on women becoming involved in business, this major obstacle is unlikely to be overcome by informal finance.

This chapter reviews informal financing methods. The relationship between informal and formal financial systems is assessed, and the advantages and disadvantages of informal sources of credit considered. Women's use of the various sources is central to this analysis.

Informal finance sources

Informal finance plays a vital role in meeting the capital requirements of the poor in most countries, in both urban and rural areas. A number of sources indicate the relatively low proportion of formal credit utilized generally in a range of poor countries (Hammam, 1989; Maloney and Ahmed, 1988; König and Koch, 1989). Most evidence suggests that the percentage of capital from formal institutions obtained by women who are establishing new businesses is lower still.

The characteristics of informal sources of finance vary according to the country and economic sector. The nature of the informal sector is determined not simply by economic factors, but also by social and political alliances and ties of reciprocity or dependence (Maloney and Ahmed, 1988; Bouman 1989). Informal and formal finance sources often coexist, although their respective market share varies. Indeed, the different financial systems are not mutually exclusive, and in practice entrepreneurs may use several methods of finance at once, or combine them with semi-formal financial sources (Bouman, 1989; Noponen, 1990). When formal finance is well distributed and adapted to local needs, informal finance tends to diminish in importance. However, because of the constraints on and characteristics of formal finance, there are always a number of needs that this sector is unable to meet and which are catered for more appropriately by informal sources.

The personal savings of investors constitute by far the most important informal source of capital for investment (Page, 1979; Kilby et al., 1984; Hammam, 1989). Another important source is the rotating savings and credit association, the Rosca. Capital is also available from supplier's credits in a variety of forms, e.g. purchase of expected production, or loans granted against a guaranteed promise of sale. In agriculture, share-cropping is common in many areas and can be a major form of credit. Other sources of credit for the poor are moneylenders and pawnbrokers. Although it is feasible in some countries to assess the relative importance of these different types of informal credit, very little of this data is disaggregated by sex. It is therefore not possible to assess their impact on women's enterprises.

In some regions, financial circuits are partly segregated by sex. There are Rosca's, for example, which only accept female members, or female moneylenders who loan exclusively to women (Maloney and Ahmed, 1988). However, in such instances the amounts of money in circulation are normally fairly small, making it difficult to break out of the vicious cycle of small investments leading to low income and savings, which in turn limit additional investment.

In some instances, substituting for expensive informal finance can be helpful to women's enterprises, and can at the same time reduce their dependency. Successful credit schemes have been designed to refinance exorbitantly expensive informal loans.[1] Money is loaned at commercial rates, permitting clients to pay off old loans and reduce the overall level of debt repayment as a proportion of their income. However, it can be difficult to reduce dependence on informal sources if for example a moneylender also controls access to raw materials, services and/or markets. Programmes that intervene in such situations must offer a consistent and full package of alternative services, while at the same time avoiding merely replacing one form of dependency with another.

Self-finance and loans from relatives and friends

Most striking perhaps is the significance in many countries of self-finance and loans provided by relatives, friends and neighbours. This source serves for initial investment, for the expansion of an enterprise and for working capital.[2] According to Seibel (1991), 'self-finance is the forgotten half in development theory'.

The absolute sums borrowed from friends and relatives generally vary by socio-economic status, and the poor normally only have access to others in a similar economic condition to their own. However, in some societies fictive kinship counters inequalities in wealth, to an extent. Thus, the Latin American *compadrazgo* system allows a poor person to establish a formal tie with someone wealthier, as a *compadre* (godparent), and this relationship may be more important economically than those with close relatives. Compadres are often sources of both employment and credit. Although frequently lending only small sums, female neighbours and relatives are another important source of finance for poor women (Maloney and Ahmed, 1988; Kuiper, 1988).

Of all financing methods, borrowing money from relatives and friends tends to be the cheapest, since they are likely to lend free of charge or at least to set very low rates of interest. This type of lending frequently forms part of a wider network of reciprocal relationships and social obligations.

Where women maintain separate finances, it may be possible for them to obtain loans from their husbands. In some regions, their husbands may even be obliged to provide an initial start-up gift (Kuiper, 1988). The degree of control a husband may exercise over his partner's enterprise if he provides the finance is an open question.

The importance of self-finance to poor women is consistently underestimated. Despite their lack of resources, the poor do save; and their savings are crucial for investment. (Bouman, 1990). Moreover, women are likely to participate more in household decisions concerning savings than in those to do with credit (Mickelwait et al., cited in Dixon, 1985).

Rotating and non-rotating funds

Rosca's originated in many areas as a type of insurance fund. In India, for example, women made payments to a Rosca in the form of handfuls of rice withheld from the household stock; this was drawn on in emergencies. Due to growing market incorporation, most Rosca's now function with money. In some areas they have become financially specialized, while in others they continue to provide a variety of services to members (Maloney and Ahmed, 1988; Kropp et al., 1989).

Rotating savings and credit organizations are found in most poor countries in both urban and rural areas. They are particularly important in many parts of Africa and Asia (Bouman, 1977; Hammam, 1989; Levitsky, 1989). In some countries Rosca's are so widespread that governments have felt it necessary to formalize them (Bouman, 1989).

There are several ways a Rosca can operate: in one of the most common, each member provides a fixed amount of money for a given period of time, which is allocated to one of the group. This member may be defined by chance, by pre-established turns, by age, by consensus, by negotiation or through bidding. For the first person in the queue to receive funds, the money acts as a loan, whereas for the last, it is more a question of retrieving savings. Some groups pay interest; the rate may be established by bidding, the person offering the highest rate of interest obtaining the loan. It is also quite common for special funds to be set apart to cover emergencies and for other services to be included. Rosca's may be organized and administered by an agent who receives compensation, but most comprise members with equal rights and obligations, often managed by a small, elected committee. Single sex and mixed Rosca's exist. Where male and female economic activities are separate, Rosca's are likely to be segregated. Typically, women's Rosca's have a smaller capital flow than men's.[3]

Bouman (1977) has summarized the advantages of being in a Rosca. Firstly, he cites their accessibility, in that anyone can set up or join a Rosca, according to her or his capacity to contribute. Secondly, he notes that the procedures are simple, inexpensive, flexible and informal and can be adapted by group consensus. Payment can be made in kind or in cash, and the period between payments can be highly variable. Membership can be shared, and the individual may participate simultaneously in several Rosca's. Another advantage is that because they do not require an office or staff and involve a minimum of documentation, Rosca's entail low, or sometimes no, administrative costs.

If the Rosca is to remain cohesive and the cycle is not to become too extended, the membership should not be too large. In many parts of the world, Rosca's average about 15 people. Large groups require more formal operations and procedures, and this means more work for board members. Also, among the larger mixed Rosca's, female participation on the board is less likely than in smaller groups.

Rosca's are often important to the maintenance of social cohesion. Normally they provide members with mutual support. Group meetings are frequently used for a wide variety of purposes and have an important social function. Rosca's also have certain economic advantages over other financing systems. For example, when interest is paid, it is low – especially as compared to that charged by other sources, such as money-lenders. Repayment is made in instalments rather than a lump sum, as with some loans. Saving is obligatory for members and may sometimes even be enforced by means of fines. In general, it can be said that informal savings become more disciplined when organized and managed in groups.

For a number of reasons, Rosca's are especially attractive to poor women. They can function with very limited amounts of money wherever interested persons are found. Payments can be made in any period thought convenient by members. Participation is free, or at least relatively cheap. Literacy and numeracy are not a prerequisite, and, as indicated, procedures and management are simple and transparent. Confidentiality can be guaranteed and funds can be withdrawn from the household economy and protected from claims by other family members. In certain circumstances, women can gain status from participation in a Rosca, since it demonstrates their economic value and strength (NIO, 1989).

Some Rosca's have additional, non-rotating, funds. These are often secured in a bank, where they earn interest. Participation in a Rosca may also provide individuals with collateral for bank loans, the stake in the fund being transferred to the lending institution. If individual members find that they are able to save increasing amounts, they are always free to join a group which makes larger regular payments.

This type of scheme does, however, have limitations. Firstly, rarely is a permanent fund established which could be used for further lending; after completing each cycle the fund is generally divided between members. To continue, therefore, it must be reconstituted. Secondly, a potential risk exists that a group may disperse before completing its cycle and before all the members have benefited, in which case some people may lose their savings. A Rosca designed to work over a long cycle will be at greater risk of failing to maintain its momentum than those operating on short cycles. However, the latter generally have limited funds.

It may prove difficult for those members with insecure or unpredictable incomes to make regular contributions. In many cases it is not possible for members to know exactly when they will receive their capital, and this makes planning difficult. A further problem is that more than one member might need funds at the same time. This is especially true when a number of members are forced to make seasonal expenditures, such as those linked with the beginning of school or agricultural cycles. In these cases members only receive their own savings back, and are unable to benefit from the accumulated savings of the groups as a whole. Finally, inflation may reduce the value of the Rosca, especially if interest is not charged, so that members who are allocated funds later in the cycle receive less in real terms than those nearer the beginning.

The problems of relative inflexibility of access are eliminated in the non-rotating savings and credit associations found in some countries (Bouman, 1989). Under this system, not all members take loans, but funds go to those with the best investment proposal or who can pay the highest interest rate. Occasionally funds may even be loaned to non-members for short periods at higher rates of interest. Savings may be accumulated at a rate chosen by individual members, and, at year-end, profits are distributed in proportion to savings – giving some savers a higher return than under fixed-rate systems. In principle, the fund is permanent, with the advantage that it continues to accumulate and provide a long term service to members.

Development programmes that aim to support Rosca's tend to adopt one of two broad approaches, either upgrading the funds or linking them to formal financial institutions. The former approach relies on the savings of the group itself; assistance is given to enable the group to acquire more members and offer more services. The latter approach promotes a dynamic relationship between Rosca savings and bank credit, with the intention of augmenting the funds available to the group (Seibel, 1991). Linking seems to have greater economic potential, in that it expands the capital base of the group. This assumes, of course, that repayment of the larger loan is possible. However, the infusion of capital in this way can generate mistrust and corruption and lead to the erosion of group discipline (Maloney and Ahmed, 1988; Holt and Ribe, 1990). Further, it is important not to put too much pressure on such groups and expect too much of them. For example, it is tempting to try and use Rosca's as a vehicle for a range of development services. But the whole idea is that Rosca's are single purpose in conception; once they come to incorporate a complex range of services, the original motivation and cohesion may be lost. Nevertheless, the experience of Rosca's has informed and encouraged the promotion of joint liability and solidarity group credit programmes globally. Undoubtedly, in countries where an indigenous tradition of Rosca's exists, there is a basis for establishing new credit schemes based on this principle.

Moneylenders and pawnbrokers

Moneylenders and pawnbrokers can be seen as specialists in financial intermediation. In some countries moneylenders are a principal source of finance (Maloney and Ahmed, 1989). Often moneylenders are expatriates, from families originally of foreign origin, or members of a special caste. For example, in Francophone Africa the Lebanese and Syrians assume the role of moneylender and in Anglophone Africa, the local Indian community. In Indonesia it is the Chinese, and in Malaya, the Chettiar – a caste traditionally engaged in moneylending – who offer this service (Adas, 1974).

Pawnbrokers also provide a considerable proportion of total credit in a number of Asian countries. For example, in Malaya they supply 20 per cent of total credit and more than 50 per cent of credit required for rice production (Bouman, 1989). The Indonesian government has engaged in pawnbroking nationwide. This source generates a turnover higher than for all their other programmes for the poor put together. In Sri Lanka, banks often have a pawnbroking window; in India pawnbrokers are licensed by the government, and in Singapore and Malaysia many pawnshops are backed by commercial banks (Drake, 1980). Loans from pawnbrokers are provided on a commercial basis and less likely to carry social obligations or be embedded in local power structures than those from moneylenders, traders or shopkeepers (Bouman, 1989).

Moneylenders and pawnbrokers may operate on a broader scale than the local level. Larger moneylenders often use agents, intermediaries or brokers, to ascertain credit-worthiness and maintain personal contact with borrowers. Sometimes financial chains exist which extend from the powerful moneylender in the city to small-scale lenders and merchants in rural communities, who loan to farmers and others locally. In some countries wealthier moneylenders specialize by serving a particular sector of the population, while smaller ones take local clients with more modest but varied cash requirements. Similarly, pawnbrokers often repledge goods with richer colleagues or with banks. These indigenous bankers clearly provide funding not only for the poor, but also for the richer members of society (Kratoska, 1975; Mahadevan, 1978).

The presence of a moneylender in the village makes access to finance easier for women because it correlates with convenient opening hours, a speedy service, no requirements for documentation, and a willingness to provide small loans. Moneylenders and pawnbrokers can be either male or female, but women's access to moneylenders and pawnbrokers is influenced by the social context. In more closed societies, women can only obtain direct loans from other women.

Societal perceptions of women generally are also very important. Assumptions about their business capacity, for example, may profoundly affect assessments of risk and this in turn determines the rate of interest they are charged. This is in spite of the fact that there is no evidence that gender determines the risk of business failure.

It is evident from the literature on informal finance that the role of moneylenders and pawnbrokers is considered highly controversial. Commonly they are characterized as ruthless usurers, or 'loan sharks', who force the poor into perpetual debt. In some cases, the same individual acts as moneylender, trader and landlord, exploiting the poor farming family at various levels.

The moneylender does, however, fulfil a function in the rural economy that is being increasingly recognized (Bouman, 1989; Kropp et al., 1989). The universal presence of moneylenders in most villages throughout the world is in itself an indicator of the level of demand for their services. Bouman (1989) notes the old Indian saying that no village is fit to live in without a moneylender, a medical practitioner, a man of knowledge and a stream that does not dry up in the summer. In practice, few other sources of finance are so rapidly disbursed, so local or so suited to small, unsecured loans.

Moneylenders and pawnbrokers tend to charge high rates of interest, almost invariably above formal market rates. But, if the full transaction costs of formal loans are taken into account, informal loans no longer appear to be so inordinately expensive. Quite apart from the delays and problems of access, in many cases the formal financial system is not prepared to risk awarding small amounts without collateral, and often bribes must be paid to obtain a loan.

A number of factors increase the cost of informal loans, including: the high opportunity costs of capital, the small amounts and short term provision made for informal loans, and the lack or insufficiency of collateral. While high interest reduces the profitability and income of a venture, it has to be recognized that paying higher than formal market rates may be acceptable for the end-user in certain circumstances, because it meets a particular need. Thus, investors are usually prepared to pay higher than average interest rates when funds are required urgently or are to be used for a particularly profitable venture.

Interest charged by moneylenders is based on a case by case assessment of costs and risks, drawing on the creditor's knowledge of the borrower and his or her previous repayment record, and taking into account the nature of the venture or item to be financed. When the borrower is in urgent need (such as with emergency health expenditures) and has few alternatives, interest may be far higher than the norm. Interest rates also depend on the form of security offered (if any). Thus, pawnbrokers charge lower interest when jewels are rendered for security than for consumer durables. They may charge higher interest than banks, but give loans up to a larger percentage of the pledged value of the security.

A key factor in the provision of informal credit is whether there exists a reasonable level of competition between the different agents engaged in moneylending at the local level. Monopolies in the supply of credit may result in levels of interest several times greater than commercial rates. But a monopoly in rural areas in particular may also be compounded by other forms of social control, as for example when the moneylender is at the same time the only commercial trader. Indeed, the moneylender may levy extortionately high rates of interest as a means of obtaining not simply the cash income, but also access to the land used to guarantee the loans. Many farmers have become landless in this way, by incurring debts ill-advisedly. In the case of monopolies such as these, development interventions can aim to increase competition and force the price of loans down (Bottomley, 1975; Wai, 1972).

Credit made available at normal commercial rates can liberate the poor from indebtedness and abuse. However, it must be recognized that when a new source of credit competes with that provided by local moneylenders, clients face certain risks because more often than not the moneylenders are members of the local elite, who may monopolize crucial services (transport, supply of inputs, marketing outlets, etc.). Thus, even though many women may use credit offered at commercial rates to pay off exploitative loans from informal lenders, they will not sever their links with the moneylenders altogether. The most rational and pragmatic solution may be for women to combine formal and informal finance (Noponen, 1990).

Moneylenders and pawnbrokers may be more accessible to women than formal banks, and they possess a wealth of local knowledge and experience. Thus it may be an advantage to integrate them into development activities. This can increase outreach considerably, without the need to invest in an expensive infrastructure and/or high staff costs. The advantages for women will depend on the extent of gender bias.

In one such experiment in Sri Lanka, informal financial institutions such as local moneylenders have been linked to banks through the Praja Naya Niyamakas (PNNs), so that the resources of the banks supplement the informal sector. The aim was to support two PNNs per village, to ensure competition and hence lower interest rates. Various financial and other controls have been adopted to guarantee that the programme meets its objectives, which include poverty alleviation (Sanderatne, 1991).

Wholesale traders and shopkeepers

Wholesale traders and shopkeepers also function as financial brokers, but this credit is linked to trade relationships. Supplier's credit is often available with an interest free grace period (up to one month, for example). Initially, purchases tend to be made on a cash basis. However, once a longer-term trading relationship is established, credit becomes available, the items purchased serving as their own collateral.

Many women engage in petty trade, and find supplier's credit to be very favourable. This system involves no collateral and requires little other investment. It would be far more expensive and complicated to execute the same operation with capital obtained from a moneylender or bank. Women often start out in business selling small quantities of semi-perishable products on credit from wholesalers, possibly seeking to deal in manufactured goods at a later stage (Kuiper, 1988). Although a relationship of trust and confidence can develop between the wholesaler and retailer, supplier's credit is still vulnerable to changing circumstances, which may well restrict its availability and continuity.

Supplier's credit is not always repaid in cash. A contract is made to sell the produce to the supplier at a predetermined price; by setting the figure at below the normal market price, an interest is exacted. When the opportunity costs of capital are high, supplier's credit is likely to be expensive. In remote areas suppliers often monopolize trade and may also control local transport. This monopoly enables suppliers to charge exceptionally high interest rates on credit.

Credit arrangements are also commonly introduced into outwork schemes, in that raw materials are delivered to the home, as a form of credit in kind. The final product is collected and paid for at a later stage by the outwork agent. It could be argued that the workers also supply credit to the company by giving their labour in advance of payment, but this aspect of the arrangement is never taken into account. Because of the exceedingly low returns to labour, such indirect credit arrangements tied to outwork – also termed contract production – can be the most exploitative of informal finance systems (Huq, 1991). Despite the disadvantages, self-employed women are often forced to make use of this system, because it reduces the need for working capital and does not require collateral.

It has been suggested that, as for moneylenders and pawnbrokers, suppliers of raw material, tools and machinery (and their knowledge of local clients) could to some effect be linked to financial institutions. This could be done by channelling funds through them. The merchant's profit would come from sales rather than credit, thereby reducing overhead – especially transaction costs – and improving credit performance. In the Philippines, for example, three official schemes target primarily agricultural input suppliers, who are used to channel lending to farmers (Floro and Yotopoulos, 1991). Obviously controls are required in such programmes to ensure that funds so directed do in practice benefit the poor. Further, women benefit only if they have and maintain credit relationships with the suppliers in the programme.

Sharecropping arrangements

In many developing countries informal finance for agriculture or animal husbandry is raised through sharecropping or joint livestock ventures.[4] It is difficult to quantify globally the role of landlords in financing agricultural production through share-cropping, but their involvement is most likely considerable. A wide variety of such contracts exists, with labour, capital and land included in different proportions. The division of investment and returns between the two parties also varies considerably. Differences in contractual arrangements in part reflect local scarcity of, or access to, the factors of production (Hogan, 1982). In some areas (in many Islamic countries for example), the proportions are defined by local custom or religious prescription, while elsewhere they are individually negotiated.

Regardless of yield or quality, the harvest is shared according to the agreed proportions, and the farmer does not remain indebted in case of crop failure. Collateral is not required. The transactions generally involve working capital only, or the purchase of livestock, and larger, medium-term investments are rarely involved. In some regions, especially where land is a factor in the transaction, the sharecropping arrangement may be very stable, lasting a lifetime possibly, or even several generations. Transactions that are mainly financial tend to be less stable and continuity is not guaranteed. Among the drawbacks of sharecropping is the fact that contracts are often made in the context of dependency relations.

Although sharecropping contracts are normally agreed by the (male) head of the household, women may engage in sharecropping independently. In countries where women have customary rights to land, the transaction may be made with their husbands or with other male relatives. Indeed, sharecropping may permit women to overcome gender-specific obstacles, enabling those with land or capital to engage in production, in activities requiring male labour.

In countries where sharecropping is considered a normal and acceptable arrangement, there is no rational reason banks and other formal finance institutions should not become involved. It makes good sense in business terms to extend such profit and risk sharing contracts to the formal sector, although certain practical obstacles have first to be overcome, such as the need to introduce sound bookkeeping procedures. In one example, the Peruvian NGO CADEP (Centro Andino de Educación y Promoción) provides women with credit to engage in sharecropping in highland potato production. This arrangement has improved the position of the women in the community and provided a sustainable credit fund (Oppenoorth, 1990). In Sudan, banks and development agencies use sharecropping arrangements and risk sharing/joint ventures to profitably expand their financial services in a situation in which traditional interest-bearing loans would not be acceptable. Other forms of risk and profit sharing by banks are discussed in Chapter 6.

Summary

a) Informal sources play a major role in financing economic activities in all developing countries, in both rural and urban areas. The major source of credit for most micro-enterprises is still the savings of entrepreneurs and their friends and families. Women have a high propensity to save, and often use indigenous institutions such as Rosca's.
b) Financial risk and reward-sharing arrangements should be encouraged. Share-cropping is less likely than traditional loans to result in perpetual indebtedness, and its persistence globally in agriculture testifies to its crucial role in rural production.
c) Informal credit has certain advantages, in that it is accessible and flexible and can cope with small sums. Informal loans are quickly disbursed, do not entail complex procedures or documentation and are arranged through personal contact. Also, loans are more responsive to client's specific needs and better adapted to local conditions. Even though gender biases may be present, these features make informal finance attractive to poor women.
d) Formal financial institutions can learn a great deal from informal finance. In the informal sector, small and short-term loans and savings facilities are readily available and collateral arrangements imaginative. Furthermore, disbursement is rapid and involves little paperwork. Possibly a case could be made for what Bouman (1989) calls 'informalizing' the formal sector, enhancing access for women and improving loan conditions and institutional viability.

Notes

1. In those cases where it is intended to reduce dependency, it is sometimes called 'liberation credit' (Devereux et al., 1987).

2. This is true not only for Third World countries. For example, in Amsterdam, the Netherlands, two-thirds of a group of 233 female entrepreneurs used their own savings or obtained loans from relatives and friends for initial investments (STEW, 1990).

3. In Sri Lanka many informants refer to Rosca's as a women's activity and, judging by the numbers involved, there are more female than male members. However, men usually pay the greater part of their wives's subscriptions and women also substitute for their husbands by having two stakes in one Rosca, or subscribing to two or more groups (Bouman, 1984).

4. Given that sharecropping is a well established system globally, the term is used loosely here to indicate profit and risk sharing arrangements in which costs and profits are shared between different people, who provide the factors of production (usually land, labour and capital) in agreed proportions. It should be added that not all sharecropping involves agricultural production.

Chapter 5

Development programmes and 'semi-formal' financial institutions

New forms of financial services, based on experience in both the traditional informal sector and the formal, have proliferated in recent years. The apparent deficiencies of existing traditional means of delivering credit to the poor – and especially to poor women – have resulted in the introduction of a wide range of new forms of provision. Some of the new credit schemes are small-scale, pragmatic responses to the problems of a specific group. In others, large credit programmes operate with rules, conditions and procedures similar to those of the traditional banking system.

It is impossible to do justice to the almost infinite variety of credit programmes in a single chapter. The discussion here is therefore restricted to a review of the most common institutional forms that have emerged as options for women.

Credit within multiple service programmes

In many development programmes – in almost all sectors, especially agriculture and community development – there is a tendency to add a credit component at some stage or other. This is largely because project managers find that the new ideas and technologies they are offering are not being adopted, as a result of the lack of finance. The addition of credit is common not only to programmes sponsored by NGOs, but also to those run by the state, or by bilateral or multilateral agencies. The project then allocates resources obtained from donors or the government to a fund, from which loans are made. Either the fund may be managed by the project, or a special line of credit may be established with a bank.

When credit and other financial services form only a minor element in a total package of services, or when they are added as an afterthought to a larger programme, certain problems commonly arise. Often credit is provided solely to facilitate other programme objectives, and insufficient thought and care is given to the financial component.

Credit, income generation and other business programmes merit special attention. When added to more general development initiatives, intellectual and managerial energy is frequently not invested in the financial element but in the main programme, on the assumption that the former will look after itself. It is not uncommon to find people with no training in financial matters, such as doctors, social workers, priests and agricultural technicians, running credit programmes, and running them badly. In these circumstances it is not surprising that the rate of failure is so high. It is possible to incorporate financial services successfully within integrated development programmes only when these services receive the professional support they require.

Development projects with credit funds generally target 'the poor', but in practice make loans primarily to men. Projects seldom explicitly discriminate on the basis of gender, but the definition of the target group often excludes most women. For instance, the landless cannot participate, or only heads of households. Sometimes credit is made available only for specific cash crops, which are produced by men. If women are not seen as engaging in productive activities, or if they do not participate in decision making related to the project, they may not be approached. In the past, women have not been explicitly addressed except by health and nutrition subprogrammes or other activities labelled as 'social and communal.' More recently, low participation of women has been perceived as a problem that must receive attention. The most common responses have been to create special credit funds for women or collective women-only income generation projects.

Short versus long-term interventions are another important issue. If credit programmes are to be really successful in improving the lives of poor people, they obviously need to be long term. A single, short-term intervention will have little impact on the economic position of the small farmer or micro-enterprise. The short cycles in which so many development programmes operate undermine the institutional and financial sustainability of credit, to the serious detriment of clients. Too often, little thought is given to continuity of access to credit after the programme ends.

A further problem is the tendency to place too many conditions and restrictions on credit. This applies to tied credit, for example. Many small-scale farmers who accept loans tied to the introduction of new seeds or fertiliser fall into serious debt. As noted, the practice of tied credit is not to be recommended, because it distorts the market and, since capital is fungible, there is no guarantee that the funds will be used as intended by project workers. While credit offered as part of a general programme may be subsidized by other activities, making it cheaper than alternative sources, this may not compensate clients for the lack of flexibility in financing.

Among the difficulties of providing credit within a programme offering multiple services is that it is often difficult to separate loan transaction costs from overall staff costs: many different roles are performed by the same people. However, because the overall number of loans is very small, transaction costs are generally very high; they are not even covered by the interest charged. Such programmes do little to improve confidence in finance. Equally, creditworthiness and repayment capacity are rarely assessed, with the result that recovery rates are frequently very poor and credit funds are rapidly eroded.

It is clear that the high rate of indebtedness in multiple service programmes is primarily due to the poor management of credit. Failure to assess market demands and constraints is common, and many programmes allow credit to saturate markets. In other cases, the poor are directed into economically unviable activities (Ministerie van Landbouw en Visserij, 1988).

The monitoring and evaluation of the credit component in general development programmes is often inadequate. Commonly, these procedures ignore crucial factors such as: the fungibility of credit; credit use; the level of real costs (including transaction costs) and benefits; arrears and default rates and their impact on financial sustainability of the fund (Ministerie van Landbouw and Visserij, 1988; Adams, 1988). In addition, many development programmes do not address the issue of gender and fail to target women.

These experiences create serious doubts about establishing credit components in multiple service programmes where no commitment is made to acquiring the specific financial expertise needed to avoid programme failure. One solution adopted by a number of NGOs has been to act as an intermediary between formal financial institutions and poor women. This model permits the financial institution to focus on management of loans, while the intermediary organization concentrates on assisting the target group and ensuring a good gender balance in the programme. When formal financial institutions are genuinely concerned to reach women's businesses, NGOs can do a great deal to help clients avail themselves of their services.

Income generating projects for women

Income generating projects may be regarded as a special form of multiple service programme, with a credit component that targets only women. Unfortunately, the performance of many such programmes has been disappointing, especially given the desperate needs of poor women, as seen in Chapters 2 and 3. As a result of the many failures in this field, income or employment-generation projects for women are now viewed with scepticism by the majority of development workers. Many of the remarks about credit funds apply in this area as well. Here, additional performance problems specific to income generating projects will be covered, to assess why these undertakings, which should be central to any strategy to assist poor women, have become anathema to so many.

One problem with a large number of income generation programmes is their use of welfare techniques that effectively impede sustainable economic development among women. Thus, while purporting to create genuine income or employment opportunities, in practice they rely heavily on subsidies from external donors. Wages paid to participants are divorced from either the real worth of their labour or the value of their production. In food-for-work and street cleaning schemes and in subsidized crafts production, for example, there is little intrinsic value in the work. Women are in practice receiving welfare payments – not wages – in exchange for their labour. It would perhaps be more honest, and certainly more cost effective, to provide cash handouts, rather than to mislead participants and allow them to think they are involved in an economically viable occupation. Any economic intervention aimed at lasting assistance for poor women must be designed to be economically sustainable and not to rely on external funds.

A second factor which leads to the collapse of many initiatives is the tendency of agencies to see economic interventions as an effective 'entry point' for working with a particular group of people. Thus, the programme is used as a way of facilitating contact with and gaining the trust of women. This approach is misguided, because it takes the women's prime objective (to increase income) as only the secondary objective of the programme. The focus by agency staff on goals – such as advocacy or organizational development – that may not be apparent to the participants, leads to the neglect and ultimate demise of the income element. Often, a tension arises between agency staff and programme beneficiaries, the latter becoming gradually disenchanted by the failure of the former to deliver promised economic improvements. Confusion concerning programme goals may also cause participants to lose confidence in themselves as entrepreneurs and in the whole idea of income generation. Moreover, economic failure reinforces the popular perception that women are poor at business.

In designing programmes for women, it is essential to understand their situations. It is often assumed – incorrectly – that women have time free to devote to additional activities. All too often, assistance is given to women to undertake new enterprises without due regard to the impact of the increased labour burden on their existing enterprise. No attempt is made to measure the opportunity cost for women of involvement in income-generating schemes that do not directly improve the performance of their major economic venture. The result is the diffusion of energy and time that might have been utilized more profitably in other ways.

Unfortunately, to compound the problem, both aid agencies and women themselves tend to concentrate on occupations such as sewing, handicrafts, raising chickens or guinea pigs, or vegetable gardening. These are often economically unpromising, characterized by low levels of profitability and poor market prospects. When asked by aid workers which activities they think should be introduced, many women respond by stating what they feel their questioners wish to hear. Their answers may therefore reflect more what the women believe agencies want, and are willing to provide, than the women's own perceived needs (Young, 1988; Slob, 1991). More often than not these projects have a negative economic performance. This situation is frequently exacerbated by agencies that encourage women to act collectively when there is no economic or social justification for doing so. Collective action is not appropriate in all contexts, and yet many programmes assume it is in some way automatically superior to individual initiative. Poorly conceived collective activities may merely accentuate women's labour burden, without providing financial compensation.

Rotating and revolving funds

Rotating or revolving funds are generally established by some external agency, and may be part of a broader development project. The external organization defines the purpose of the fund. In these plans, a given amount of capital is loaned out to a group or individuals under formally established conditions.

In a revolving fund, *capital* revolves: every time payment is completed, the same member can take a new (sometimes higher) loan. In a rotating fund, after the capital loaned out to a member is repaid, it is loaned to another in the group. The borrowers rotate; only when the whole cycle is completed can members obtain credit again. Potential borrowers are generally clearly defined – that is, some form of group membership is required. Rules and loan conditions vary a great deal. Revolving or rotating funds that mobilize savings perform better than those that operate only through credit (Kropp et al., 1989).

All-male rotating and revolving funds exist, as do those with mixed membership, or with the family as a whole as one member. Women-only rotating or revolving funds have also been established. Unfortunately, little detailed information on gender-related differences in performance is available.

Revolving funds serve only their members, but membership may increase as a fund grows. A problem of rotating funds is that improved access for any member is only temporary, and is followed by a long period of non-access before a new loan is possible. On the other hand, rotating funds generally do not require collateral, while revolving funds may do so: a common phenomenon is that old members feel entitled to claim some security from new members – so they, in case of failure, will have this collateral to help make up for their losses. This could restrict access for women, since they often possess less collateral, and their entrepreneurial capabilities may be perceived as less good or reliable than those of male producers.

In general, rotating or revolving funds receive some type of support from NGOs, or other intermediary organizations. They often are managed by these supporting agencies, but in some cases they (after an initial period) are self-managed. Rotating or revolving funds are considered to be more easily adaptable to target group needs than banks, because of their local scope. The member is also not at the mercy of a bank or other distant lender. This can be essential for continuous production within his or her enterprise. They may function either as an independent activity or within a development project context.

Normally the scope of rotating and revolving funds is small, but they are highly replicable, for instance to neighbouring communities or others with similar conditions. An organization or movement that organizes and stimulates replication may be highly effective. Donor grants deposited in a bank, making interest available to begin new funds, could also stimulate replication (Kuiper, 1989).

For the intermediary institution or the fund, costs related to credit tend to be low. Interest, or a fee to cover costs and risks, is normally charged. Once provided with capital, theoretically the funds require few reserves; if well managed, they can grow or expand their capital base. However, many funds have lost their capital. Erosion of the fund can be due to high levels of default, but may also be due to interest charges that are too low, so that administration costs and/or default risks are not covered.

Inflation is a second major threat to these funds. High levels of inflation may drastically reduce the value of the fund or of the loan to members who receive their capital towards the end of the cycle. Under such circumstances, the fund is more like a lottery than a business; those receiving loans early in the cycle are the winners, and those who receive them later, the losers. Sometimes a guarantee deposit is required in hard currency, to help maintain the capital base in the face of inflation.

Loan repayments depend chiefly on social control and discipline. Members of a fund are expected to know each other. Arrears influence revolving velocity negatively, increasing costs and affecting the fund's capital. Therefore there may be, for instance, fines. However, arrears tend to be lower where premiums are paid for timely repayment (Perano and Pössinger, 1987).

Revolving funds tend to have lower default rates than rotating funds because the member has a more individual stake. But in rotating funds group pressure is a strong incentive for repayment, at least where sufficient group cohesion exists, because members who have not yet received a loan will insist on repayment (Perano and Pössinger, 1987). Women prove to repay more reliably than men, and the poor more so than those who are better off. Political control over a fund has a negative influence on financial performance (Kuiper, 1989).

In revolving funds, credit mainly serves to finance working capital. Rotating funds are more to be recommended for investment, although the longer repayment cycle for bigger investments reduces rotation velocity. Revolving and rotating funds can operate with money, or with credit and repayment in kind. Seed funds are the most common example. (Administration costs are however high.) Capital goods can also be delivered within a rotating context. Normally some sort of leasing or hire-purchase construction is chosen in this case (Du Marchie Sarvaas, 1989).

Within either revolving or rotating funds, the fund may be transferred to the group after an initial period. Generally though the group is in charge of very little, mainly performing tasks to facilitate the functioning of the bank or programme and carrying part of its costs. In fact, however, effective member control over the funds in self-managed rotating and revolving funds is the only guarantee that the organization will not switch to policies that do not serve the interests of the members, and will act in a more or less appropriate way with respect to practical details. In self-managed funds it is very important that the capacity for administration and control is not limited to a few members, since creating opportunities may eventually lead to fraud. Moreover, all members need sufficient insight and assertiveness to understand the accounting.

This is often a problem, especially in women's groups. Women have lower levels of literacy and numeracy, and may be too shy to speak out. Often only a few women have the knowledge, willingness, and ability to exercise control. Men are sometimes asked to participate, to perform these functions, but this of course can lead to other problems (jealousy from other men, monopolizing the discussion and perhaps group policy setting, opposing interests, etc.). These factors can also deny women effective participation in funds with mixed membership. Conversely, many rotating and revolving funds have proved to be good educational opportunities, for technical training as well as training in business administration or handling capital. Participation in educational activities is sometimes a prerequisite to membership and obtaining loans.

Rotating and revolving loan funds have several advantages for women. Firstly, being situated locally, they are accessible. Secondly, loan conditions and membership forms can easily be adapted to the women's particular needs. Thirdly, joint liability renders collateral less important. Finally, the funds can be self-sustainable and, as suggested, are easily replicated.

Savings and credit unions and cooperatives

Since the late 1950s, savings and credit associations, sometimes founded by organizations and movements of poor people, have become common throughout the world. Initially, these associations were a marginal and mainly urban phenomenon, but their accumulated experience and aggressive, mostly politically-inspired, strategies of expansion have helped them become significant mobilizers of savings throughout the world. The movement has been further supported by government policies, and by church and NGO involvement.

At present there are some 60,000 savings and credit associations globally, with roughly 80 million members, of whom more than half are situated in the Third World (Marion, 1990). A significant proportion of the lower and middle classes in many urban and, to a lesser extent, rural settlements are involved; in countries such as Argentina and Peru these associations mobilize the greater part of national privately-registered savings.

Credit and savings organizations of this almost formal type, with a regional scope and unlimited affiliation, have usually been established by external agents. Most are now relatively independent of their founders, though, and can usually guarantee meeting the needs and interests of their members. Many have additional social functions, such as providing health, funeral and life insurance.

Cooperative boards, who are elected by the membership, are responsible for policy development. In most countries the board is both restricted and protected by national law. Even with these controls, the members/borrowers are able to exercise influence over the organization. There are exceptions in some countries, though (such as India and Bangladesh), and a number of associations – in contravention of cooperative law – are controlled by a political party and are used for political patronage, undermining their financial viability and democratic image (Bouman, 1989; Maloney and Ahmed, 1988).

Trust, solidarity and mutual support are required not only to obtain loans secured by group liability, but also to sustain the additional services, such as insurance, that are normally provided. In most cases, support services for credit operations are also available to members. A strong feeling persists that, on the whole, the cooperative bank is a far more responsive institution than the large and inaccessible commercial banks that generally serve the rich, and has the added advantage in most cases of being locally based. Moreover, the cooperative bank promotes the local investment of capital, instead of its transfer to other areas.

The savings component is a major element distinguishing credit and savings cooperatives from formal banks. Indeed, it is through their savings that members become committed to the institution: the borrower's stake in the organization is greater even than in revolving loan funds or development projects with a credit component. Whatever its size, the saved capital serves as a base for further fund raising and converts each of the contributors into a creditworthy client.

Individual savings serve as leverage for the provision of credit in different ratios to the amount accumulated (1:3, 1:5, 1:10, etc.). Under the most common system, the loan is guaranteed by the savings of the person contracting the loan, as well as the other members. The onus is on the borrower to identify members with sufficient savings who are prepared to assume joint liability for his or her loan. In turn, other members can ask for a reciprocal guarantee for any loan they may contract. Thus only part of the total loan portfolio of the credit union is actually covered by member savings. Normally a ceiling is set for this type of credit and the amount obtainable is directly linked to demonstrated savings capacity, against which possible repayments are set.

Here too, continuity of credit is guaranteed because a member can obtain new, and often larger, loans once repayment on outstanding debts is completed. Loans for larger investments are, however, generally restricted by the ceilings stipulated by unions and cooperatives.

Loan conditions vary considerably. For example, associations that serve employees tend to be based on monthly repayments. A wide range of maturities and repayment schedules exist, including some very short-term loans with daily repayments. Since profit is not the prime aim, interest is normally kept as low as possible and credit is relatively cheap when compared to other sources. Normally there are few conditions on the use of loans by members. However, larger investments may require monitoring, and in cooperatives that limit membership to a specific group there may be restrictions on the purposes for which loans are allotted. Thus, for example, credit unions based on a company, a trade union or a syndicate mainly provide loans to meet consumption and housing needs.

The delivery systems of credit unions and cooperatives often resemble those of formal banks, although the former are generally better adapted to their members and usually employ simpler procedures. The bureaucratic requirements tend to increase, though, when government interference in the running of unions or cooperatives is extensive. One major challenge is to extend the outreach of these organizations into rural areas. Often it is too costly to maintain a presence in rural areas and at the same time provide access to all potential clients. There are some solutions to this problem, including the deployment of agents to collect savings, or use of mobile or temporary offices. A further difficulty here is the need to accommodate the unreliable and seasonal nature of cash flow in rural areas in savings and repayment schedules.

In the main, the credit available from these organizations is provided out of savings mobilized locally. In regions where there are few banks, credit unions can mobilize hitherto untapped savings. Thus, integration into national and international financial networks and agreements with the formal banking system can provide access to further sources of capital. This increases the liquidity of associations with a capital base too narrow to satisfy all credit and finance needs. Unions and cooperatives generally have a good record of financial sustainability, although there have been losses in some countries due to bad management. Transaction costs tend to be lower than in the formal banking system and default is rare because of the guarantees given by the joint liability groups. Default rates may be high, though, in those cases where government or party political interests prevail.

While savings and credit cooperatives have certainly helped poor men obtain access to finance, it appears that women have not benefited to the same degree (although their participation rates are not as well documented as men's, and so it is difficult to be precise on this issue). Steps need to be taken to make these associations more accessible to women, since many still operate under discriminatory rules. For example, the procedures for obtaining loans usually require applicants to be literate, thereby seriously limiting the number of poor women who can avail themselves of the service. Despite such shortcomings, the lending and savings policies of the cooperatives impose fewer barriers to women than formal banks.

In most countries, it is likely that if sufficient women were to become members, and to participate in the decision making process, discriminatory rules could be removed. For example, if opening hours were to be adapted to women's daily routines, delivery systems improved and procedures amended, this would make the associations far more useful to female members. There is still a great deal of potential for poor women in the credit union and cooperative movement.

Peoples' banks

The past decade has witnessed the emergence, particularly in Asia, of specialized financial organizations with a poverty focus. A number of these organizations, such as SEWA (Self Employed Women's Association) and the WWF (Working Women's Forum) in India, have been created specifically to serve women. In addition to banking facilities, they often provide a number of support services, the most important of which are training in business skills, such as the management of credit and savings, business management and marketing.

The origin of the peoples' banks is varied. Some emerged from situations in which NGOs performed an intermediary role between banks and poor clients, where separate financial institutions developed due to frustration in dealings with the banks. Others began as small credit programmes, some targeting a specific social group, which then expanded. They have tended to become more specialized financial agencies as they have developed, and also to offer a wider spectrum of credit and related services. The relative success of many of these schemes has encouraged major NGOs such as BRAC (Bangladesh Rural Advancement Committee) in Bangladesh and Sarvodaya in Sri Lanka to launch large credit programmes as an adjunct to their ongoing work. Some of the older and more established peoples' banks now have a membership of over 100,000. Many have acquired the character of movements, with all the key decisions being made by the membership and the overall programme being guided by moral principles, permitting them to represent and express the interests of members nationally and lobby for policy change.

Success is demonstrated not only by size, but also in terms of good repayment rates and the degree of participation by the poor. Some of the organizations restricted to women have tens of thousands of members and excellent repayment rates. Many with a mixed membership have also succeeded in attaining very high levels of female participation, largely through careful targeting.

At the outset must be mentioned, however, that the non-commercial objectives of the banks (including a commitment to assisting the poor) can create financial problems. Further, most of these institutions depend on donor funds or discounts from central banks for their survival. Thus as a result, while there is no imperative to make a profit on individual loans – enabling the bank to support people who would not otherwise obtain credit – overall profit levels are low. At the same time, delivery, training, monitoring and transaction costs for small loans are very costly. Programmes that deal exclusively with small loans are unable to meet costs and produce a profit, and thus cannot achieve any significant internal cross-subsidization.

Dependence on donor funds and central bank discounts threatens the sustainability of the peoples' banks, exposing them to political vagaries and policy change. The vulnerability of peoples' banks and need for greater financial sustainability is of increasing concern both to the organizations themselves and to their donors. Financial and institutional sustainability can only be achieved through economies of scale, and such economies imply both a reduction in costs relative to the number of loans issued and an overall increase in loans. If a wide range of other support services are also provided, there is likely to be a continuing need for external funding.

The structure of the peoples' banks is similar in some ways to the savings and credit cooperatives, with the crucial difference that they are mostly local initiatives and not ruled by international standards as are cooperatives. Moreover, they draw their inspiration directly from the financial experiences of the informal sector, and experience gained from earlier credit schemes.

The various successful initiatives in this area share a number of characteristics. The goal – to provide financial and other services to the target group, whether this is defined as all poor people, or just poor women, or women in a specific geographical location or trade – is very specific. Another common feature is that the delivery system is adapted to the specific needs and constraints of the target group. Gender-specific constraints can thus be taken into account. For example, if the target group has only limited mobility, branches will be small and located nearby. Working hours and visits to homes or businesses will be scheduled to suit the clients.

Attention is paid to improving the self-confidence of clients. Thus, local languages are used whenever possible, procedures are quick and straightforward, documents simple and transparent, and staff are recruited from the local population. Special measures are taken to enhance women's participation, including the employment of local women as staff, the training of male personnel to be sensitive to the circumstances of female clients, and promotion of a relaxed, informal atmosphere in branch offices. The quality and dedication of both staff and management are important features of these programmes, regular staff training is common, and incentives are offered to ensure the quality of service.

The use of joint liability or solidarity groups has been one of the most important developments in these organizations. Joint liability groups can be an effective and least-costly way to reduce defaults on loans and to mobilize savings. Successful groups are characterized by mutual confidence and coherence; the way the group is organized is crucial. Self-selection, for example, whether according to neighbourhood, activity, class, caste, or gender, is vital. The size of the groups will also influence their performance; some organizations prefer small groups, of 5 to 10, because they allow for more personal relationships to develop; others promote larger groups to expand their capital and savings potential and reduce transaction costs. The optimum size and character of a group will probably depend ultimately on the local culture and conditions.

Groups discuss the functioning of credit, and appraise business proposals and credit applications. The assumption is that members know each other well, and thus also will know how to evaluate proposals and whether repayment is likely. Groups generate peer pressure; this acts as a control on investment and repayment, since access to funds for individual members depends on repayment by the others. The groups also facilitate loans by reducing transaction costs for lenders – although in part this is by transferring costs to the borrowers – and reducing risks to the bank (Huppi and Feder, 1990). Too, they channel information and provide a forum for training and exchange visits. Some groups benefit from non-financial services, such as health and education. Some organizations expect members to engage in a lengthy process of learning and group participation and to demonstrate savings discipline before allowing them to take out loans. In the short term, group building can be costly for both lender and borrower.

Group functioning is illustrated by these remarks on the Grameen bank:

If someone wants a loan, the bank asks her to find four more persons who also need loans. Then these four must find two or three more. Together they form the group, which then can gain confidence and discuss the business problems and prospects of each member. To determine poverty, land and housing are taken as a standard. In rural areas you cannot hide – the group knows you, whether you are poor and whether your business proposals are real and realistic. Then, over seven days, every day the members meet or are visited. Everybody must bring in a certain amount of money every day. After a few days the question is raised: how would you want it to be protected, etc. Sometimes an existing group is brought in, to explain their experience. Then, when a cohesive group has been built, it is decided who will take a loan from the bank and for what activity. (Huq, 1991, personal communication.)

The question is often raised as to whether or not such groups should consist solely of women or contain both sexes. If the groups are indeed self-selected, the problem is not for the bank to resolve, but for the women themselves. Experience has shown, however, that in the initial phase particularly, it can be more convenient to form separate groups for women and men. Segregation of the sexes facilitates communication within the group and, of course, protects women from male monopolies, giving them the opportunity to become board members or group leaders and acquire crucial administrative and management skills. As a group matures and starts to develop complementary functions, it will more likely meet the interests of its female members if controlled and dominated by women. Another advantage of having groups containing only women is that they are not obliged to seek permission from male relatives to engage in loan transactions.

When a group is composed exclusively of women, it offers members the special opportunity of meeting each other, gaining confidence and courage and becoming

involved in decision making (Arunachalam, 1991). This is an effective way of addressing strategic gender interests (see Appendix 1) within the framework of financial
interventions. Of course there is a risk that groups consisting only of women will be
perceived merely as a focus of social activity and of marginal economic importance,
and thus receive little attention. Ultimately, women have to be encouraged and helped
to also become active in mixed boards and structures in order to defend their interests.

One problem is that self-selected groups may exclude very poor members, or that, in
groups that are not economically homogeneous, prejudicial attitudes against poorer
members may tend to develop. Thus, many groups seek to exclude the poorest altogether, out of fear that they may not be able to repay their debts and will therefore limit
overall credit availability (Maloney and Ahmed, 1988).

In one programme, pressure from both the intermediate organization and other
members of the group, who were eager to obtain new loans, made it impossible to re-
schedule loans for women who faced a crisis. It was possible to maintain high repayment rates only because group leaders or other members covered for defaulters; women
perceived as risky borrowers were gradually forced out of the group. Almost half of the
women involved – particularly poorer women with few reserves – eventually lost
access to credit (Noponen, 1990).

Policies on loan use vary among peoples' banks. The Grameen Bank, for example, has
adopted a policy of non-designation in the distribution of credit; decisions are made for
the member's convenience, as agreed by the solidarity group, regardless of whether the
loan is to be used for trade, capital, investment, production or consumption. By employ-
ing this approach, the bank has provided loans for over 500 different activities (Huq,
1991). The credit offered by the Working Women's Forum, on the other hand, must as
a matter of policy be used for investment. However, in practice half of the loans
provided were used in ways other than intended by the agency (Noponen, 1990).

The amounts loaned are largely determined by the expectations of the loan officer
and the joint liability group with regard to the member's capabilities and the viability
and nature of the proposed venture. Often an upper limit is imposed, set mostly in
relation to the member's savings.

Terms of repayment are short – rarely extending beyond either one year or a single
production cycle – and rather rigid. Some organizations have created systems which
allow for frequent repayment of small amounts. Only in the case of loans for housing
and land are longer repayment periods accepted. These limitations tend to make it
difficult for members to take out loans for larger investments, which could allow them
to become more productive.

Interest varies a great deal and the rates are usually similar to those of the formal
market, but lower than those of the informal. Differential rates often exist for different
credit lines and activities. And, unlike formal banks, the peoples' banks tend to charge
higher rates of interest for larger loans than for smaller ones, reflecting the scarcity of
capital rather than the cost of transactions.

Among such organizations there is a wide consensus that traditional collateral is not
critical as a guarantee for repayment. A number of measures are commonly adopted to

reduce risk in the absence of collateral. These include: tying the amount loaned to the member's level and rate of savings; introducing savings schemes that give the borrower a stake in the organization; using borrower's groups for joint liability; conducting detailed appraisals; exercising moral pressure; and making further loans conditional upon repayment. Genuine defaulters will always exist, but – unless repayment policies are exceptionally rigid – a solution can usually be found to their repayment problems. Wilful defaulters seem to be rare in these programmes and default rates are consistently lower than in other more traditional credit schemes. It should be noted that in peoples' banks the repayment rates of poor female borrowers are particularly high (Holt and Ribe, 1990).

Many of these organizations pay considerable attention to the mobilization of savings. A strong savings base can help the long-term financial viability of the organization, in addition to providing a good indicator as to which clients are likely to be able to repay loans.

Most such banks have established a form of member ownership, mainly organized through shareholding. Ownership by members is meant to guarantee that the institutions will operate in the interest of the clients. Some have special arrangements (such as one member, one vote – as opposed to one share one vote) to ensure democracy, and others have rules concerning the sale of shares. In the Grameen Bank, for example, there is a built-in control mechanism ensuring that women will maintain their majority: if a woman sells a share, it must be to another women, whereas if a man sells, it may be to either a women or a man (Huq, 1991). When women are elected as representatives by the members, they may become participants in developing the policy of a peoples' bank.

For their members, these organizations offer more than just the economic opportunities provided by savings and credit facilities: they also provide the potential for mutual social and economic support and a vehicle for political and economic lobbying. In some cases these banks have become important pressure groups at the national level, lobbying for changes on behalf of women on matters specifically related to financial policy. The existence of credit organizations for women and of women's pressure groups helps to define and articulate the interests of women with respect to finance.

Some organizations consider advocacy and lobbying on behalf of members to be one of their main objectives. This is the case of the Indian organization, SEWA, for example, which:

not only...actively supported women's enterprise, but has also organized women to become effective pressure groups at the local, national and international levels. These pressure groups have lobbied effectively for women as legitimate clients of the nationalized banks; for women's legitimate space in municipal markets; for women as suppliers of various goods and services required by government programmes; for the application of formal sector labour laws and benefits to informal sector workers; for maternity, life and occupational insurance schemes for women; against cases of harassment or exploitation of women workers; and for other measures of public recognition, support and protection of women entrepreneurs. Perhaps most significantly and fundamentally, SEWA has effectively lobbied for the legitimacy and representation of self-employed women in the international trade union movement. (Chen, 1989, pp. 143–144.)

Peoples' banks have been able to help large numbers of poor people by stabilizing their employment and income. A proportion of members inevitably become successful repeat loaners; many will eventually want to expand their activities beyond the capacity of the lending programme. They then require a different service, such as special credit lines or loans from banks, which permit graduation to a higher level of economic operations. It has been commented, however, that as yet such credit lines have still to be created (Mobassar Husain, 1990).

Throughout the world, schemes based on the peoples' banks, especially the Grameen approach, are being implemented. Formal financial institutions and large-scale donors are also considering how they can emulate the model by scaling down their current services to provide for small enterprises. And client-led approaches are becoming more common now that it is clear that the provision of financial services to poor men and women is not only feasible but also makes sense economically.

Summary

a) The addition of a credit component to development projects dedicated to other aims is often an appealing option. However, badly planned credit interventions do not help anyone. Management, sustainability and overall impact must be carefully considered from the outset. It is important to have expertise available before starting credit schemes.
b) Collective income-generating projects for women are rarely economically viable; they tend to remain marginal. The women involved seldom earn significant extra income, although their labour burden may increase. These projects often embody contradictory objectives, to the detriment of economic feasibility.
c) Rotating and revolving funds can provide limited but useful services to women. If well managed, the funds can be sustainable. Accessibility of these funds for women depends on their membership policy and procedures. The more influence and control members have over the fund, the more likely it is that it will be adapted to real needs. Revolving funds seem to offer a wider scope than rotating funds, because the emphasis is on making the best use of the money rather than on rotating member access to the capital. The major risk is erosion of the fund, due to default or inflation.
d) Savings and credit unions and cooperatives have the advantage that they mobilize their own capital and are more or less democratic. Small businesses and savers are not excluded from membership. Participatory methods help ensure that these organizations meet the real needs of members. Demonstrated savings capacity and joint liability are used as security against default, rather than formal collateral. Members can obtain new, and often larger, loans once they have established their creditworthiness and repayment capacity. The gender bias present in the wider society is also reflected in the cooperatives, but the potential to challenge this bias exists and, with some adaptation, a useful service can be provided to women.
e) Peoples' banks have proved to be one of the most successful ways of making financial services available to poor women. They have adapted delivery systems and loan conditions to meet the specific needs of (female) clients. They have flexible repayment

schedules and use joint liability groups rather than collateral. Members can obtain new and larger loans once repayment is completed. Transaction costs are relatively high, if the costs of confidence building and other support services are taken into account, but default rates tend to be low and poor women have excellent repayment records. Some have been able to mobilize members and lobby for improvements in their positions. Many of the features of these organizations could well be introduced into any finance programme; their principal drawback is dependence on continuous external funding, mainly to cover support services.

f) Finally, thousands of experiments with revolving funds, credit programmes and savings and credit organizations have taken place, creating an invaluable pool of experience. It remains vitally important to ensure that NGOs, grass roots organizations and other development agencies disseminate information about such experiences to all who can have an impact on improving the access of poor women to credit.

Chapter 6

Women and the formal financial system

On the whole, the formal financial system has failed to provide appropriate services to poor women, and remains committed to an extremely narrow range of clientele. This chapter discusses the formal financial system and describes in some detail the main obstacles encountered by women seeking credit from formal institutions. It also analyzes various approaches which could serve to resolve these problems, effectively meeting women's credit and other financial requirements. Many of the solutions outlined are based on the successful experiences of semi-formal financial institutions and on informal sector practices.

Formal financial institutions and poor women

The formal financial sector consists of banks, mortgage companies and other financial institutions. Formal institutions are usually subject to the rules of a central bank and regulated by national, or sometimes regional, law. They specialize in financial operations and can, in principle, mobilize almost unlimited financial resources. The formal character of their dealings is intended to provide a safeguard against fraud and default, although the persistence of financial scandals in many countries illustrates that there is no absolute guarantee against such crimes. While it is usually assumed that banks are effective and efficient providers of financial services, capable of handling large numbers of clients, this is not always the case.

Private commercial banks obtain their funds from various sources, including shares, savings deposits and borrowing from a central bank or other institutions; profit is their central objective. To maximize profit, they target those markets and clients thought to provide the highest rate of return for the lowest level of cost and risk.

Since commercial banks are generally only to be found where costs are not prohibitive and demand is sufficient to justify their presence, they are absent from many rural areas. In order to compensate for this, governments established in the past a large number of public sector agricultural development banks – frequently with financial assistance from the World Bank. These institutions were largely intended to promote agriculture; it was expected that, in keeping with this aim, they would channel funds to small farmers. Credit was often provided at subsidized rates. Strict conditions on the use of loans were imposed and loans were frequently tied to specific purposes and purchases. The poor performance of the agricultural development banks is now widely recognized and is discussed in some detail in Chapter 1.

Public development banks have also been involved in financing small-scale enterprises outside agriculture. Institutions that offer credit to small-scale enterprises on the basis of minimal extra services and interventions seem to have performed somewhat more successfully, because they have based their programmes on past experience (Levitsky, 1989; Boomgaard, 1989). However, many of the large capital funds, such as some of those sponsored by the World Bank, have still not benefited very small enterprises significantly: their management has been too centralized, they have demanded excessive documentation and a level of financial accounting not available in small-scale enterprises, and have often established rules against the provision of working capital (Levitsky, 1987; Devereux and Pares, 1987; de Jong and Kleiterp, 1991).

When development banks and some commercial banks have attempted to target credit programmes to the poor, they have in most cases failed. Rarely did the poor benefit in practice, and less still were women assisted. The experience of the peoples' banks described in Chapter 5 shows, however, that banking for the poor is a real possibility, and that formal institutions should be able to offer appropriate services to women without compromising their other goals. Further, poor women have good repayment records and a low default rate. This should provide sufficient incentive for commercial banks to seek alternative clients from the large and often untapped market comprising small enterprises.

Given the constraints on using grants to fund credit for large numbers of women, access to large-scale private capital is the only long-term solution for sustainable financial services. One strategy for encouraging mainstream institutions to open their doors to female clients is to reform and adapt existing bank procedures and practices. Organizations such as Women's World Banking have been created for this purpose. Their intention is to demonstrate to banks that women make creditworthy and profitable clients, and to remove obstacles to their becoming such. It is argued that by confronting gender issues, pressure can be brought to bear on the banks by middle class and wealthy businesswomen; if gender bias is resolved, poor women may also obtain access. Once gender obstacles have been overcome, the only remaining problem for poor women is banker's reticence to extend credit to small enterprises or to those that lack collateral, plus the high cost per transaction in relation to the size of the loans involved.

The strategy applied is to have organizations act temporarily as a bridge between potential female clients and banks. The organization acts as an intermediary, helping to fit the financial needs of women to bank procedures and requirements, and teaches women how to deal with banks. The object of the exercise is not only to provide loans to women but also to convince banks that women are creditworthy. However, in this approach, banks do not need to adapt, and do not learn directly about their new clientele's requirements and problems. A major related problem is that bank staff are not sufficiently challenged by contact with clients to review policy and practice, unless training is provided. Moreover, it has been found that once intermediaries withdraw their support, banks often cease to deal with female clients. Thus, 'in terms of seeking to reorient mainstream capital markets, experience in trying to encourage banks to be more responsive to poor clients has so far been discouraging. Banks' goals, structure and orientation appear to work against meeting the needs of this clientele' (McKee, 1989).

Some observers doubt that banks are capable of lending directly to poor women. 'Transaction and management costs of banks, in particular, could threaten their survival, because the economy of low-income rural households cannot generate sufficient business volume to sustain them' (Bouman, 1990, p. 165). Given the scale of their enterprises, poor women will be at a particular disadvantage in dealing with banks that are concerned about transaction costs. Such factors will be further exacerbated in rural areas, where, as indicated, population density is often insufficient to maintain local branches of commercial banks. Despite these difficulties, there have been numerous attempts to increase the outreach of commercial banks. It is felt that even if only a portion of new clients accepted by banks were poor women, this could still significantly expand the credit facilities at the disposal of small businesses, given the resources available to formal institutions.

It is clear that very few banks are willing to take the initiative of offering their services to small farms and similar enterprises, least of all those run by women. Most banks are very conservative. Few have the vision to encourage new customers from non-traditional areas of the economy, in anticipation that they might in the long-term make considerable profit from the more successful of these. In general, banks that have been obliged to work with the poor have discontinued the relationship once the incentives or legal obligations have been removed, even when rates of default have been low and repayment high.

When banks do choose to innovate and extend their services to the poor, as part of a strategy to expand their client base, they can be encouraged in a number of ways. Support can be given, for example, in the form of incentives, such as subsidies for staff training and institutional adaptations, temporary discount facilities on loan funds to cover extra costs and guarantee funds to meet additional risks. Monitoring will be required to ensure that these services do indeed reach the intended beneficiaries. (Delgado, 1991.)

There is also some potential in institutional arrangements which exploit the comparative advantages of banks and intermediate institutions: some programmes, such as IDESI (Instituto para el desarrollo del sector informal) in Peru, are serving thousands of clients. For example, a bank may deal with all aspects of financial administration, while an NGO provides follow up services and ensures that social targeting is effective. It is sometimes possible to use external funds for such programmes, but care needs to be taken not to become totally dependent on external donors. In the final analysis, one of the main objectives of these schemes is to encourage banks to allocate their own funds to new clientele, and establish a system which is sustainable once external support is withdrawn. The one major question under this division of functions is who will pay for the services provided by the intermediate agency when such support is not available, since here intermediary services are no longer perceived as short term support.

A wealth of recent experiences testify to the many ways in which women can avail themselves of services offered by the formal banking system (see Chapter 5). As poor women's bankability becomes more widely accepted, it is important that lessons from experiments worldwide inform future decisions about the way finance institutions and poor women can work together.

Barriers and possible solutions: a challenge to banks

Savings
Provision of formal savings facilities is one way of paying interest and giving women access to credit at the same time. Formal savings schemes can adopt one of two approaches: they can make available secure deposit facilities in which savings earn a real rate of interest; or, in the absence of collateral, a proven history of savings – demonstrating the financial prudence of proposed clients – can be established so that it can be used to obtain credit. This latter approach works on the basis that a history of regular savings is generally regarded as an indicator of the capacity to meet loan repayments. Unfortunately there are a number of major problems with formal savings schemes. For example, the outreach of most formal banking institutions is extremely limited, especially in rural areas. Moreover, few encourage small deposits and most either pay very low rates of interest or none at all.

One of the strategic errors made by a number of development banks has been to depend on external donor funds, neglecting local capital obtained via savings deposits. The failure of many such banks to flourish can be traced to this weakness. Another problem is that existing savings schemes, both public and commercial, have tended to channel funds from rural to urban enterprises. In the main this is because of their failure to match savings services with credit provision in rural areas. There is thus clearly scope for establishing appropriate savings schemes linked to provision of credit.

While formal savings systems facilitate the release of credit, it should be remembered that there are many informal ways in which people with small sums can save effectively, such as the many indigenous savings schemes, or savings circles, run by groups of women on a collective basis (see Chapter 4).

Outreach
In most countries formal banks have branches only in towns and villages close to major communications networks. Because of women's reproductive obligations and restricted physical mobility, services must be provided close to the home or workplace if they are to be useful. The time and expenditure absorbed in travelling to a bank can increase the cost of borrowing considerably, especially for women living in rural areas.

Improving outreach implies that banks will incur additional costs, and this will only be acceptable to the institution if the promised turnover of the new branch justifies such expenditure. As mentioned in Chapter 5, some relatively low-cost models have been developed for rural areas, such as mobile offices using cars, jeeps, or even motorbikes. Another approach is to open branches on a part-time basis. Agents can be hired to work for the bank on commission, collecting savings and loan repayments daily, or serving as intermediaries for credit applications. The commission is proportional to the amount collected and thereby provides the agent with an incentive to maintain good repayment and savings rates. To avoid the risk of misappropriation of funds by agents, they are often required to leave a considerable deposit with the bank as a guarantee (Bouman, 1989).[1] Outreach can also be improved by involving other intermediaries in a similar way.

In many countries the post office is the institution with the greatest network of offices distributed nationally, and has trained staff who are accustomed to dealing with cash. Post office savings banks already mobilize considerable savings, but have not been adapted to provide loans. There are a number of new proposals to develop post office banking to its full potential: this should be possible with only marginal additional cost.

Confidence building

If they wish to attract more female clients, commercial institutions will have to overcome their very negative traditional image. Poor women's experience of banks and other such institutions has been very discouraging, and this will not be easy to redress. At the moment banks seem to go out of their way to place hurdles in front of new clients, and seem to feel under little obligation to sell their services.

To overcome this hostile image and the lack of confidence most poor women have in them, banks must improve their communications. First, it is important to allow branches the flexibility of responding to local needs and conditions, rather than being inhibited by centralized procedures and decision making. Once a clear picture of local needs is available to a bank, an appropriate strategy for reaching women can be identified. Information on what the bank has to offer, how it works, the requirements for obtaining credit and rules concerning repayment and default must be made available. Methods of information dissemination that combine mass communication with direct targeting of women's groups and individuals have proved successful in a number of countries. To realize such a strategy, it may prove helpful to use intermediate organizations.

Delivery system

The delivery systems of many banks are not conducive to conducting business with women. Administrative procedures are often complicated and the volume of documentation is intimidating. Many women have received little formal education and as a result have low levels of literacy and numeracy. Bank documents are often difficult to understand and are seldom available in local languages. Bank opening hours are particularly inconvenient for women, and staff are often prejudiced, having little understanding of the problems faced by their poorer female clients. Internal bank rules and national legislation further discriminate against women.

The result is that poor women generally find they must pay several visits to the bank to arrange a loan, and may find it difficult to obtain funds to pay for bank commissions, legal costs, bribes and travel. The real transaction costs to the borrower can be so high that it is cheaper to seek a loan from a moneylender. The difficulties of approaching banks also lead many women to delegate financial transactions to male partners. This reinforces both their dependence on male relatives and the popular perception that they lack firmness and assertiveness (Angeles, 1991). As indicated in Chapter 5, however, peoples' banks have shown that it is possible to make delivery systems more accessible to women: procedures are simplified; they are quick and require little documentation.

Staff are locally recruited and their training has equipped them to deal with women's financial needs.

Use of loans and loan conditions

The conditions on which loans are made available must correspond to the needs and priorities of poor women. If the conditions imposed on the use of loans are severely restrictive, their value to women is greatly reduced. Other chapters have already indicated the drawbacks of credit tied to specific packages of inputs and crops that are not a priority for women. In general, the fewer the conditions set on small loans and the greater the choice in the use of funds, the better. Moreover, loan conditions should be adapted to women's working environment, allowing if necessary for realistic maturities; repayment schedules set according to cash flow; debt rescheduling adjusted to repayment capacity; and daily repayments. (UCE, 1988.)

For loans to be well serviced it is necessary to establish the capacity of women to repay, but not to question how the funds will be used (Huq, 1991). Joint-liability groups can be involved, to carry out appraisals. The implication is that loan appraisal can be less standardized and rigorous than at present.[2] Rather than a detailed balance sheet indicating a woman's income and expenditure, it is probably more useful to have a clear idea about the dynamics of the economic sub-sector in which her enterprise operates. To work effectively with micro-enterprises and small farms managed by women, it will be probably necessary to retrain bank staff in such procedures (see Chapter 5).

Repayment and debt capacity

In the popular perception, formal credit is often viewed merely as a mechanism that penalizes the poor and forces them to deliver up their assets, because of harsh penalties on default. Stories about people who lose their home, land or cattle, because they are just a few days overdue with repayment or a few pennies in debt, are common. In practice, however, most banks try to avoid foreclosing on a loan and seizing collateral. Indeed, there are numerous examples of development banks and others who, for political or charitable reasons, cancel debts or do not insist on repayment. However, this policy can cause certain problems. Borrowers often only discover later that new loans are contingent upon repayment of these old debts. And when one institution allows clients to default, repayment discipline in other credit programmes locally tends to decline markedly.

Informal credit arrangements are often open ended, and generally a solution can be found if terms defined at the outset cannot be met. The formal sector tends to be more rigid in this respect and may have difficulty in changing repayment schedules, especially for small loans, with the result that women who fall into arrears may be forced to turn to other sources for help in making repayments. Inflexible repayment schedules and the popular perception that banks may seize assets pledged as collateral make women extremely reluctant to seek formal bank loans. Yet indebtedness, used appropriately, may be necessary to the financial health of an enterprise. It is not indebtedness that causes problems, but the possibility of creating debts that cannot be serviced.

To allay fears of using credit, banks should develop approaches aimed at accommo-dating clients, solving problems and allowing for the rescheduling of debts and, where appropriate, for further credit to be given to assist this latter process. Increased credit may sometimes be essential, to provide working capital and meet consumption needs, so that production can continue. If interest rates can be kept low, the debt capacity of clients increases. Longer repayment periods have the same effect. The best way to im-prove debt capacity, however, is via an increase in productivity or income.

Risk reduction

Risk insurance
To reduce the risk in loan agreements to both female clients and formal lending institu-tions, one good solution should be to tackle the problem of production and marketing risks. One of the major sources of economic uncertainty for poor women is the problem of price instability. It is particularly difficult to predict prices when the market is mono-polized (which is often the case in developing countries) or when the product is highly perishable. When there are seasonal and other regular trends, it is possible over time to calculate these and therefore to develop insurance policies to compensate for major market swings (Hogan, 1982).

Climate, insect plagues and disease in many areas account for the vulnerability of agricultural production. The poor are more affected by such factors than the wealthy, because their land is generally more marginal and they are less likely to have access to irrigation and other technologies that might counteract changes in weather conditions or remedy disease. Although climatology now allows for a greater degree of sophisti-cation in predicting change in weather, such advances rarely reach the poor.

There have been several attempts to insure against climatic damage to crops, but these have proved to be costly and require high premiums to cover the employment of specialized staff for damage assessment and other functions. Less costly, however, are schemes which use insurance as a substitute for collateral, where only a proportion of the value of production is insured – that proportion being sufficient to meet repayments on a loan. Costs are reduced by limiting the insurance to the production cycle and inves-ting premiums in income-bearing accounts. In areas where levels of risk and vulnerabil-ity are particularly high, and premiums would also most likely be very high, an alter-native might be the creation of risk or profit sharing arrangements.

Risk sharing arrangements
Credit is not always the most appropriate means of financing small enterprise, especi-ally when the risks involved are not easily quantified. Activities that are new and experimental for both women and the financial institution can be particularly difficult to gauge. An alternative method for funding such activities is by using venture capital, which allows for rewards and risks to be shared and flexibility to be introduced into financing. The aim is to augment the capital of an enterprise by increasing the equity. This is done by issuing or selling shares which are bought by the financial institution.

The bank and the entrepreneur become business partners. Sharecropping or raising animals jointly are in essence alternative forms of joint enterprise (see Chapter 4).

In developing countries, formal experiences with venture capital are relatively new. Those venture capital companies that do exist tend to specialize in a given sector, product, technology or clientele (Popiel, 1990). Venture capital may prove a useful mechanism for women who are engaged in viable economic activities but lack capital. Banks should consider collaborating with women on such a basis.

Venture or risk capital is especially appropriate for agriculture in situations where high levels of risk in some years are compensated by high profits in others. In risk and profit sharing arrangements, farmers are not required to be property owners, since their labour input can take the place of land. Venture capital is also used for non-agricultural activities.

Since in venture capital arrangements all costs are discounted before profits are shared, the transaction costs are not especially high for the bank. The relationship between lender and borrower is crucial with this form of finance, and interdependence between business partners helps increase mutual confidence. The introduction of risk/ profit sharing on a large scale requires banks to make certain adjustments in the way they work, to enable them to cope with contracts which are almost individually negotiated. One of the main differences between credit and venture capital is that in the latter, the bank or other capital source assumes the role of co-manager, rather than controlling the enterprise.

Banks are unlikely to become involved in venture arrangements that entail large amounts of capital and long repayment schedules, because this would tie up their own capital too much. They therefore tend to seek investments which are low risk and provide a fast return. This makes venture capital especially appropriate for short-term financing or working capital – which is what agricultural and small and micro-enterprises most need. For longer-term investments based on profit sharing, it is necessary to ensure that the bank can withdraw from the arrangement by converting outstanding debts into a more conventional loan.

Venture capital, in order to best serve both parties to a contract, must be flexible. When giving farmers credit, banks traditionally ask for repayment to be made immediately after the harvest – a time when prices are low. However, in profit sharing arrangements it may be in the bank's interest to adopt a different policy, waiting for prices to rise (perhaps even financing storage costs) before demanding a sale.

One of the greatest advantages of venture capital is that if the enterprise fails, the business does not become indebted to the bank. To work well, contracts based on risk and profit sharing must be backed by good accounting and bookkeeping.[3] Small enterprises may need support to comply with this requirement. Without such procedures, it is impossible to establish the true costs and benefits of the enterprise.

In some countries present legal structures prohibit venture capital and similar such operations; therefore it may be necessary for alternative legal and institutional forms to be introduced before such models can be adopted (Delgado, 1991).

Since Shari'a law opposes the use of predetermined interest, profit sharing has been long established as an alternative form of credit provision in Islamic countries. Islamic banks have evolved a wide variety of arrangements and terms, with different forms of investment and profit, special procedures for short and long-term investment and for coping with failure and loss. The systems commonly employed include: murabaha (hire purchase), musharaha (a type of risk sharing or venture capital) and mudaraha (similar to sharecropping). The experience of Islamic banks could prove informative in complementing traditional forms of sharecropping and developing new forms of profit and risk sharing finance within the formal sector (Iqbal and Mirakhor, 1987; Zineldin, 1990).

Collateral arrangements and guarantee funds
Traditionally, banks try to reduce the risks incurred in making loans by insisting that the client make collateral available, which can be repossessed in case of default. Poor women find it difficult to provide hard collateral because they have few resources. Often, for example, they hold usufruct rather than ownership rights over key assets such as land. Moreover, joint household property such as land or houses is generally registered in the name of the husband. This means that women are less likely than men to benefit from mortgages, for example, given their more limited ownership of assets that can be used as collateral.

A number of semi-formal financial institutions have developed alternatives to collateral, such as joint liability groups, or guarantees co-signed by non-borrowers (see Chapter 5). Other methods (as discussed elsewhere) include pawning, hire purchase, leasing, profit/risk sharing, sharecropping and insurance of client's credit with the bank by a specialist insurance company.[4]

Guarantee funds are another approach being used to persuade banks to provide credit for poor women and men. Money is deposited, either by an organization or the government, with the bank itself or in a holding account elsewhere. This serves as a guarantee in case of default on loan repayment, thereby reducing the risk to the bank (Women's World Banking has often used this method).

Normally, the value of the guarantee fund is far lower than that of the total loans authorized. This is because the aim is to guarantee the calculated risk to the bank of its new portfolio, rather than to cover all the loans individually. It is generally felt that a guarantee of 10–25% of the total lent is sufficient. If we assume that repayments from poor women are in fact very high, then the risk is correspondingly low for both the bank and the institution providing the guarantee. A relatively modest guarantee fund can therefore make available much larger sums from the bank (Jacklen, 1989).

The fund must be established with an agreement setting out the respective obligations of both the bank and the guaranteeing agency. At the very least, the agreement should detail the conditions under which the fund can be called upon; outline a programme for the guarantee agency to gradually phase out its support; and note who is to benefit from any interest. To keep defaults to a minimum, it is also important to ensure that bank procedures are appropriate to the type of business envisaged. It should be made clear that the bank has the responsibility of being as vigilant with loans covered by guarantee as it would be with other loans.

To cover any losses incurred in meeting bad debts, the fund should be invested in an interest-bearing account. One important fund, which provides guarantees in many developing countries, is operated by RAFAD in Geneva. This organization, as a matter of policy, does not deposit money in the banks where it provides guarantees, but maintains its core fund with a major international bank with a reputation such that it encourages other banks to participate in the scheme also.

Where guarantee funds are deposited in the loan-granting bank, in many cases the interest accruing from the guarantee funds provides an incentive for banks to become involved. However, this makes it difficult to phase out guarantees, even when poor women show themselves to be creditworthy, because of the marginal profitability of their business to the bank. Thus sustainability is unlikely.

Other alternatives

A policy aimed at assisting clients to accumulate their own working capital is the ideal alternative to collateral. Where local conditions do not permit such a policy, caution is needed to avoid the saturation of a small enterprise or farm with credit.[5] A stepped credit strategy, offering alternative forms of credit, would be most effective in avoiding dependency on credit or a serious imbalance in the debt/equity ratio. Various alternatives to credit exist for such situations, including rent, hire purchase, leasing, and mortgages. These systems enable women to obtain the means necessary for production or consumption without taking credit, or using their assets as collateral.

Renting enables small businesses to gain access to items they cannot justify purchasing. While collateral is not normally needed for renting, sometimes a guarantee is requested to cover possible damage. Hire purchase is a very popular alternative form of credit, in that machinery and other capital inputs purchased with the loan can be used as collateral. Hire purchase can only be used in this way if the enterprise needs capital inputs that can be resold in case of default. It does not give access to working capital. Too, problems can occur when the cash flow is erratic and does not facilitate regular payment.

Leasing is a very common form of credit in many parts of the world, but has yet to be adopted on a large scale in developing countries. Leasing can be compared to renting, but the maintenance and other costs of the object in question are provided for by the lessor, and the lessee does not usually become the owner. Leasing can be used by small and micro-enterprises to obtain access to tools and machinery or other non-circulating capital. Since the asset is self-secured, leasing is another way of overcoming a lack of collateral.

Mortgages are common in the purchase of land and housing, and can be used to obtain other larger items with a medium-term life. Again, as with hire purchase, the asset acts as its own collateral. Normally cash flow and income information will be required by the bank before a commitment can be made to such an arrangement. The institution may also insist that insurance policies be taken out both for the item being purchased and against the life of the client.

Support services

Improvements in the procedures and accessibility of financial institutions alone may well not lead to an increase in applications for credit by poor women. As noted, many women are not familiar with the way banks function and are uneasy about approaching them. It may be necessary to make additional support services available to encourage women to make use of the new or improved credit facilities. Time must be devoted to assisting women to prepare bankable proposals and explaining how the system works, for example (Arunachalam, 1991). Other support services, such as training in management and administration, marketing, or technology, may also have an important impact on the development of the small enterprise and its effective use of credit.

It is tempting to design large, integrated and comprehensive interventions as a solution to the many problems faced by women in their business activities. A word of caution is required, however, as programmes that try to confront all these obstacles are generally extremely expensive and cumbersome to manage, absorbing a considerable proportion of the resources of both the support organization and the small business. Before becoming too involved in the provision of support services, an effort should be made to identify preexisting resources and local networks women can use. The introduction of a new credit programme will, however, almost invariably require a degree of support and follow-up, even if for only a short period. Support services require specialized personnel; sometimes such expertise is not available in traditional financial institutions, but must be provided by intermediate agencies.

Basic training may be required to improve literacy, numeracy and other skills among women. Information will also need to be disseminated about government and bank procedures relating to small businesses and training in bookkeeping, administration and marketing will most likely be popular (Rajagopalan, 1991).

Opinions concerning the value of training for the development of small enterprises vary widely. Some observers regard training as essential at all stages, while others argue that it only has a role when targeted; still others believe it to be completely superfluous. A USAID (United States Agency for International Development) evaluation of micro-enterprise programmes revealed that training and technical assistance for small enterprise development has a very poor record and concluded that business training may be helpful, but not without more research and experimentation (Boomgaard, 1989). Furthermore, Levitsky (1989) and Harper (1989) hold that there is no hard evidence that beneficiaries of programmes which combine credit with training and/or technological inputs perform better. They therefore doubt the effectiveness of such schemes.[6]

On the whole, training linked to business development – whether offered by official agencies or NGOs – has a bad reputation. The educational and pedagogic methods used have been of low quality and inappropriate to client needs. Women's needs in particular have been poorly catered to in the design of training programmes, and gender bias has therefore not been eliminated. Rather than being designed to meet demand, training is often made a prerequisite for receiving credit, with the result that courses are held in unsaleable skills. Training should respond to demand and be designed specifically to assist clients to overcome the obstacles to the development of their enterprise, rather than follow the preconceived ideas of trainers, which may have no bearing on reality as experienced by the clientele. Alternative and informal approaches have been insufficiently explored by development agencies, and schemes based on apprenticeship or on-the-job training should be given greater consideration (Harper, 1989; Grierson and Latowsky, 1992).

Women who are trying to run small farms and enterprises will undoubtedly have a range of training requirements, which can be met partially through informal channels and partially through institutionalized programmes. For training to be cost effective it should be well targeted to women's needs and economic activities. If not well planned or executed, training programmes can absorb a great deal of money without having much impact.

Transaction costs and incentives to banks

Transaction costs are probably the most important factor impeding the access of poor women to credit and savings facilities. As indicated, high costs incurred by banks in servicing small loans and savings accounts are a major disincentive to their expanding services to this group. Women are particularly disadvantaged, because their loans and deposits are on average smaller than those of men. A bank will be under pressure from shareholders not to expand their portfolio to include small accounts that provide only marginal revenue. Even non-profit institutions cannot afford to enter transactions whose costs exceed the interest or income received from the loan without endangering their financial sustainability.[7] The need to reduce transaction costs is a major issue for those banks and semi-formal institutions that have adopted a client-led approach. If costs are not kept to a minimum, it becomes impossible to continue to offer services designed to meet the needs of the poor, or to convince major commercial banks to expand into this market.

High interest rates can compensate for high transaction costs. The Bank Rayat Indonesia (BRI) is one institution that has adopted this approach. Experience with subsidized credit interest schemes that were subsequently transferred to market rates (KUPEDES, in Indonesia, is an example) indicates that many small borrowers – male or female – are not deterred by the resulting high interest rates, so long as they receive the loan within a reasonable time, and without having to resort to excessive bribery (Seibel, 1991). However, if the rates are too high, the number of clients served by the programme will be reduced, because the financial viability of projects decreases proportionately with increases in interest.

A more effective way of coping with this problem is to reduce the transaction costs by improving the productivity of banks. Streamlining and simplifying procedures and introduction of computerized technologies to speed up administration can make a great deal of difference. As stated elsewhere, transaction costs to the bank can also be reduced by transferring them to borrower's groups, which then undertake tasks such as loan appraisal and collection of savings and repayments (see Chapter 5). Specialized intermediate organizations also have a role to play in this area, although here too trans-action costs are not necessarily reduced, but simply transferred from one institution to another: the services of the intermediary still have to be paid for.

Savings and credit services can be accompanied by other services that are more profitable, thereby compensating for the low returns from the basic accounts. Packages may for example include a combination of savings, credit, insurance and accounting services to reduce overall costs. However, it is important to note that cutting costs in this way is more feasible in more differentiated urban settings than in less developed rural areas (Delgado, 1991).

Discount facilities are another way of reducing the impact of high transaction costs and providing incentives to banks. These are funds loaned at subsidized rates by donor organizations to banks and other institutions such as peoples' banks and cooperatives. Central banks sometimes lend to commercial banks at a rate of interest a few points below the current market value, to enable the latter to either direct funds to certain specific sectors of the market or subsidize interest rates to clients. Many international financial institutions and donor organizations have provided discount facilities to banks and development projects; it is clear that it is only because of such 'cheap' funds that many banks have opened credit lines for women's small and micro-enterprises (Zapatos, 1991).[8] Discount facilities have also been given to support consolidation of financial institutions. For example, accessibility to banks for poor women can be facilitated by investments made in simplifying procedures, improving outreach, training bank staff and hiring female loan officers.

There is no single strategy for reducing the transaction costs involved in making credit available to small-scale borrowers. As we have seen, various methods can help in this regard, but in any given situation it is probably necessary to introduce a mixed package of measures which together reduce costs. Given the problems involved in changing banks, it is likely that for the foreseeable future alternatives to traditional formal banking will be required, if small borrowers are to receive credit.

Long-term access to and sustainability of financial services

For many clients, the reliability and continuity of access to credit is far more important even than cost. If a credit programme is to meet the real and long-term needs of small enterprises, it is essential that it is both sustained and continuously available. There is, however, very little evidence that programmes designed to provide a single injection of credit into small enterprises have a longer term impact.[9]

While organizational sustainability may relate to many other factors, financial sustainability is basic. There are certain key principles to achieving such sustainability. For example, most banks use interest payments to cover their costs (including those associated with borrowing, administration, arrears and default and support services, as well as compensation for inflation). Interest must be sufficient to cover costs even when subsidies or discount funds are phased out. Financial sustainability is more likely when a bank's portfolio includes large loans, rather than small ones alone, and when interest rates are high. There is therefore a trade-off for financial agencies between sustainability and enhancing access to small loans.

Financial institutions that operate in situations of hyperinflation, which is having dramatic effects on credit provision in a number of countries, have particular problems. High rates of inflation make normal banking almost impossible, and in this situation credit for small enterprises is one of the first services to suffer. Whether credit services are managed by commercial banks or semi-formal institutions, the tendency in such economies is for interest rates to lag behind inflation, thereby reducing the value of the credit fund.

Most credit programmes that operate during periods of high inflation only survive by obtaining subsidies. Such funds are sometimes obtained through grants or soft loans. Many institutions subsidize their customers in hyperinflationary economies and as a result make a loss. Others have been known to survive by using their position in the economy to speculate: buying and selling commodities in short supply, and making profits by exploiting the upward price spiral.

As long as the transaction costs of small loans are higher than the income produced by interest, poor women will only obtain access to credit by utilizing the subsidized services of intermediary organizations, or by means of other subsidies, whether on interest rates or given directly to lenders. For a small number of women, business will flourish, and the size of their account will make them attractive to banks. However, the majority of women will remain vulnerable to changes in donor and government policy and support. Once subsidies and other forms of support are removed (as is likely to occur sooner or later), the problems of high transaction costs and low profitability will once more emerge. Credit programmes for poor women therefore run the risk of being among the first to be cut when overall costs have to be reduced and profitability increased. Thus, it is important that considerable attention be paid to creative designs that permit cost effective financial services to be developed for poor women.

Where women are not seen as potentially profitable clients for commercial banks, they may need to rely on political influence to ensure continuity in the provision of financial services. This clearly suggests a need for mobilization and organization of self-employed women. It is, further, unlikely that poor women will become very influential within commercial banks. They are more likely to acquire power and to be able to ensure that institutional services are appropriate to their needs within peoples' banks (see Chapter 5).

Client participation on the boards of development banks, however, will probably not assure genuine responsiveness to poor women: it is difficult to select board members who are truly representative of the clientele, which after all is not homogeneous. It is also difficult for board members to avoid being co-opted by the institution in which they operate. Further, women as a whole are far less likely to be represented on such boards than men.

In commercial banks, decision making is normally linked to share ownership. Women rarely possess shares, and those who do are unlikely to represent the interests of poor women. In certain circumstances, grass roots organizations, such as unions, trade associations and intermediary NGOs, may be able to exercise influence, representing member interests within the financial sector.

The performance of financial institutions

Despite the importance of good monitoring and evaluation to the planning, execution and management of credit programmes, there is a shortage internationally of evaluations in general and of impact evaluations in particular. Very few evaluations question whether the financial needs of poor women, specifically, are being met, or what impact the programme has on their needs and bargaining position. Instead, most evaluations are concerned more with programme performance than impact.

Some of the reasons for this are seen in the debate concerning the criteria which should be used to evaluate credit programmes. Adams (1988) argues that evaluating the impact on borrowers is not feasible, because the results are too diffuse, too subtle and involve too many heterogeneous actors to permit accurate measurement. He favours instead focusing on the way these projects affect financial institutions.

Yaron (1991) suggests that not only self-sustainability, but also degree of outreach in the targeted population and the size of loans granted could be used to gauge whether small enterprises are in practice being served by the programme. The degree to which a financial institution is self-sustainable can be reviewed by analyzing on-lending rates, deposit interest rates, loan collection and administration costs. Outreach, on the other hand, can be assessed by looking at women's participation, the value and number of loans and savings deposits, the variety of services offered, the number of branches, and the percentage of total rural population served.

Most evaluations fail to take all these factors into account, and only register the percentage of women who participate and the rate of loan repayment. On the other hand, participation of large numbers of women in a credit and savings scheme does at least indicate that it is accessible and acceptable to women. But evaluations need to move beyond this, and look at the differences in levels of participation between women and men, and at the factors influencing these different degrees of participation.[10]

Rates of repayment can be used in evaluations to indicate, on the one hand, whether loans are being made at a level borrowers can afford and, on the other, whether clients are creditworthy. As mentioned in earlier chapters, the few programmes that record gender-specific data indicate that poor women have excellent repayment rates (Holt and Ribe, 1990). Repayment rates do not, however, provide an insight into who receives the loan or how it is used (Levitsky, 1989).

Further, repayment rates are highly susceptible to 'creative' bookkeeping, since many different methods of calculation can be used. Programmes may calculate the number of loans overdue in relation to all outstanding loans, while some assess loans overdue in relation to outstanding loans on a yearly basis. Others only take into account the loans that it is certain cannot be recovered at all, but ignore payments that are over-due, even when recovery may not be possible.

Summary

a) The potential impact of access to formal financial institutions for poor women could be considerable. The experience of the peoples' banks indicates women could make effective use of new services, if these were offered by the formal sector.

b) The current objectives, structure and orientation of most formal financial institutions severely limit the access of poor women to their services. The results of interventions that have sought to stimulate commercial banks to lend directly to poor women have been disappointing.

c) Increasing women's access to financial institutions is important, in part because they can provide continuity of access to credit. But effort is needed to find sustainable ways to continue services to this group.

d) Long-term involvement of intermediate organizations that perform a broker's role between poor women and banks can be useful, but if costs are not covered by the interest paid, such arrangements may not be sustainable financially.

e) Banks can only lend effectively to poor rural women if they develop a client-led approach, which entails removing procedural barriers, improving outreach, and adapting loan conditions.

f) It is necessary to investigate ways of reducing the risk, to both banks and borrowers, which is inherent in credit provision.

g) Small loans will always imply relatively high transaction costs; it is therefore important to reduce these as far as possible, to make working with small enterprises more attractive to banks. A trade-off exists between financial sustainability and enhancing access for those who need small loans.

h) Monitoring and evaluation of credit and savings programmes for women need to be improved, and indicators appropriate for use in these reviews to be further developed.

Notes

1. It is suggested that moneylenders could perform services for formal banks that are similar to those of an agent. However, the lender's private business interests may conflict with those of the bank (Chapter 4).

2. However, the Northern Mindanao Development Bank (NMDB) noted that their software specialist could not cope with the existing variety of loan forms and conditions in their small enterprise credit program (Delgado, 1991).

3. The introduction of bookkeeping in sharecropping arrangements may present difficulties. For example, it is difficult to ascertain exact costs of production, and labour time is particularly difficult to

calculate. Reaching agreement in advance regarding the system of bookkeeping to be used is essential, to avoid disputes over calculations of costs, labour, and other inputs.

4. Instituto Libertad y democracia in Lima, Peru, provides an example of insuring clients' credit.

5. Theoretically, the capital used to finance production costs must earn a profit which is at least equal to the interest to be paid, with a margin to cover the average production risks. The higher the proportion of production costs financed by credit, the higher the interest burden and the smaller the profit in average years (or the higher the losses in bad years and thus the higher the rate of credit saturation).

6. On the other hand, apparently one-third of entrepreneurs assisted by the Carvajal Foundation in Colombia, after reviewing their business plans with the Foundation, decided they needed training (Carvajal, 1991).

7. Thus, for example, no bank will be able to afford to charge only 24% interest on a 200,000 Rps. loan, when the transaction costs are 50,000 Rps. (Seibel, 1990).

8. Easy access to discount facilities can, however, reduce the incentive for a bank to pursue the relatively more costly strategy of increasing savings deposits. In the long run, this can threaten the financial sustainability of the bank.

9. Programmes may assume that giving credit once is sufficient to assist poor people. This is believed to allow borrowers to accumulate sufficient capital to meet future needs, making further credit provision unnecessary. More often than not, though, a one-time intervention does not allow for accumulation, so that any subsequent change in the enterprise or the economy that generates a need for additional credit will force entrepreneurs to return to traditional sources.

10. In one urban lending scheme in Peru, only 16% of borrowers were women. An evaluation showed that the major obstacles to women related to the collateral and documentation required, which were more stringent for women than for men. Loans were not made in the trade and services sectors, where women predominate. The relatively large average loan size was a further indication of the limited participation of poor women (Buvinic and Berger, 1990).

Epilogue

Before ending this book, we return to a question that should be central: whether savings and credit schemes are effective for poor rural women. We need to know not only whether credit schemes are apt to meet the immediate financial needs of poor women, but also whether they are relevant to long term 'strategic' interests – that is, whether they are seen as making a positive contribution to women's decision making role and bargaining power. Unfortunately, however, there is not a great deal of information available about impact in these areas.

The few existing reviews of the impact of credit on women deal in the main with changes in income and productivity. A number of evaluations do show that providing poor women with financial services can significantly raise income and productivity, while also reducing the hours they work (Holt and Ribe, 1990). Others conclude that credit has enabled self-employed women to stabilize their employment and income, thereby increasing their economic security. Still others show at least a moderate increase in income (Bhattacharya, 1990; Berger, 1989; Chen, 1989; McKee, 1989; Noponen, 1990). Those women who were able to benefit from a series of stepped loans tended to slowly expand their activities, move into new and more profitable lines of work or build up their savings (McKee, 1989; Noponen, 1990).

Most evaluations of the impact of credit on women's income have noted positive changes in the status and respect accorded women. Many also note that women experience an increase in self-confidence as a result of participating in such programmes. These changes seem to be due both to the higher incomes earned by the women and to their involvement with institutions and participation in borrower's groups. Some programmes even became a catalyst for mobilizing women collectively on their work problems, and on a range of other specific gender issues (Chen, 1989; McKee, 1989; Noponen, 1990).

Though too many factors related to the impact of enhanced access for poor women remain unexplained, the indications are thus positive. It is quite possible that the many innovations being developed and replicated in this field, in which gender issues are taken seriously, are making a difference for those poor women who obtain access. However, without profound and careful evaluation of programme performance and impact, it is hard to demonstrate this or to compare the merits of various approaches.

Planning financial interventions

Though assessments of effectiveness remain in the province of needed future research, in this book we have explored the complexities of financing women's enterprise. We have concluded that access to financing is difficult at present, and that what is available is often not well suited to use by women. Even in the absence of better information about what types of programmes would be most effective, however, it is possible to see certain general principles that must be considered in designing interventions, whether for use by banks or other organizations.

At present, many multipurpose development programmes offer credit; some explicitly target women. However, only a few services are offered (commonly tied credit), and availability is often short term. If services are to become significant in the long term, mobilization of savings and access to mainstream capital funds will be needed. Effective delivery of financial services requires specialization, expertise and continuity. Thus programmes should either make a commitment to developing the needed expertise, or find ways to work with the formal system.

Opening the doors of the formal financial system to poor women is the alternative to special credit programmes, and is an appropriate long term goal. But thus far, even though poor women have very good repayment records, interventions aiming at encouraging banks to accept them as normal clients have resulted in few changes. Only a few innovative banks have taken up this challenge.

Where banks are not able or not prepared to deal directly with poor women clients, organizations that have a record of effective work with poor women can serve in an intermediary role, between the bank and women clients. In this way, the specialized knowledge and expertise of banks and intermediary organizations can be combined, and can enhance access. In such programmes, institutionalization of the relationship and cost recovery for the services of the intermediary are major issues.

Local circumstances can justify the creation of financial institutions, parallel to mainstream organizations. This might be necessary, for instance, where formal financial institutions are absent or refuse to consider lending to poor women, even when offered incentives and guarantees. The presence of an effectively operating parallel institution may sometimes lead to a restructuring of the formal financial system. However, a major problem in creating such institutions is access to funds for lending and to provide sustainability.

In designing any new institutional arrangement, it is necessary to build in a considerable time horizon and to aim for structural change. Any relatively short term programme that makes no provisions for continuous access is bound to have a limited impact. This implies a structural commitment to services for poor women and that institutional sustainability will become a major concern. The value of loanable funds must be maintained and even expanded; costs must be covered by the interest margin. There is of course a trade-off between financial sustainability and enhanced access for women clients who need small loans, given the high transaction costs involved. Therefore it is likely that subsidies for institutions will remain necessary in the short run, but these should not be used to subsidize interest rates for end users directly.

The goal should be to reach large numbers of poor women who want access to adequate financial services. We argue that a client-led delivery system, adapted to gender specific constraints, is needed, and that this requires a profound knowledge of poor women's activities, and potential and constraints of specific groups of women. Too often programmes have failed because of false assumptions and lack of information.

Understanding the local situation also requires assessing the relevance of financial services, the extent of needs, and debt capacity. For example, the role played by savings in the area must be investigated. Further, given the importance of informal financing, it is important to review its scope, methods used, attributes and limitations before planning new services. It is also important to look at macroeconomic factors, especially the way they impact those sectors in which women are heavily involved.

Carrying out a general assessment of poor women's needs and the context of their work nevertheless should not require indulging in several years of preliminary research. It should however involve people and organizations with local knowledge, including proposed beneficiaries, in collection and review of data. They should also play a part in programme preparation and implementation, beginning in the early stages.

Involvement of those with local knowledge, including beneficiaries, is particularly important for an additional reason. In planning programmes it is necessary to remember that often poor rural women, or their relatives and acquaintances, are apt to have had experience with saving and credit schemes. These experiences may not have been positive, and yet will determine local expectations and opinions on any new programmes. Gaining the confidence of the women involved is a vital task, which must be undertaken before any intervention can succeed. Early involvement is a positive step in this direction.

Finally, flexibility, creativity and experimentation are among the most important factors in designing, developing and delivering financial services for poor rural women. Choices must be made in the initial stages of implementation, and the consequences of these choices will be difficult to foresee. This means that some room for experimentation will be necessary as the programme develops. Nevertheless, clear objectives with respect to the groups of women to be served, and a plan for the programme monitoring and evaluation must be built in. Programme performance, including changes in women's access, is an important focus; the impact on women's enterprise, living conditions and position in the society – the larger context of women's interests – is equally important. If impact cannot be measured directly, useful indicators must be developed. Such evaluations can eventually provide the data needed to increase the effectiveness of savings and credit programmes for poor rural women.

Appendix 1: Gender

Gender is a concept that refers to learned, culturally determined (as opposed to bio-
logically determined) differences in the behaviour patterns of women and men in
relation to each other and to their social context. Activities, rights and obligations are
considered feminine or masculine by a given society or social group; members of that
society learn to play gender roles in accord with these expectations. The norms and
values that create gender roles are present both in society as a whole and in the household. Gender roles greatly influence the position of women and their prospects in life.

Gender roles affect the division of labour; they also affect access to and control over
the allocation of resources, benefits, and decision making. This contributes to interdependence between women and men, which is complex, subtle, flexible and involves
power relations. It also has implications for women's income generating opportunities.
Women often have less access to resources than men, and less control over their own
labour. Access to certain sub-sectors and sources of employment may be restricted, and
support services may be harder to obtain. Finally, they may have difficulty exercising
control over their income.

Gender-specific characteristics are thus important variables to consider in planning
and policy making. The impact of gender, however, is modified by other socioeconomic variables, such as socioeconomic status of the household, ethnicity, and age.
Gender roles vary within a society and over time; 'women' are not a homogenous
group. Acknowledgement of this heterogeneity by planners is crucial. Women differ
with respect to work, interests, and needs.

Meeting women's needs

While a growing body of research and information now describes the roles of women
and men in many different situations, there is little consensus on the nature of women's
difficulties, the solutions needed, or the specific impact that economic change has on
them (Young, 1988). Policies that target rural women are too often based on assumptions, ignoring the broader development context. There is also considerable ambiguity
over the broader redistributional issues raised by assistance to poor rural women
(Kandiyoti, 1990).

A framework is needed to make possible the identification, assessment and prioritiza-
tion of the needs of women. This must be based on an acknowledgement of their heterogeneity. One approach is to distinguish between women's condition – their material
state, including poverty, excessive work burdens, and lack of access to resources; and
their position – their social and economic standing relative to men (Young, 1988).

This distinction between condition and position leads to a differentiation of practical
gender needs versus strategic gender interests. The practical gender needs of women
(and men) derive in part from their need to provide a livelihood for themselves and

their families. They must accomplish this within the roles allocated to them by the gender-based division of labour that prevails in their society. A credit project, for example, that needs to identify practical gender needs can ask women what their 'felt needs' are. These are directly experienced in daily living conditions. Nevertheless, the assumptions and project traditions of both women and programme planners regarding each others' possibilities and problems can easily interfere with the expression and interpretation of felt needs.

Strategic gender interests are related to the need of women for a milieu that allows them to be self-confident, to articulate their views, and to acquire more say in decision making, an improved negotiating position, plus access to power structures; and if they so choose, to organize themselves to strive for structural social change. Strategic gender interests, unlike practical gender needs, cannot be observed; they must be deduced by analysing the position of women in a given society. This involves making ethical and cultural judgements about equity and social justice. Both who makes the analysis and specific local circumstances will influence the results of such an analysis.

An improvement in the condition – the everyday circumstances – of women is very much needed. But improvements cannot become sustainable without an accompanying improvement in women's overall social position: that is, before women have more recognition and a greater voice in decision making. Concomitant attention to strategic gender interests is vital. Interventions must therefore deal with both practical gender needs and strategic gender interests. Identification, assessment and priorization of potential interventions must begin from these premises. There is, however, no blueprint to supply concrete measures that will achieve the needed improvements. A new analysis must be made for each specific situation. How best to meet either practical gender needs or strategic gender interests will vary with local circumstances (Grown and Sebstad, 1989; Young, 1988; Moser, 1989).

Appendix 2: Symposium participants

Sharing poverty or creating wealth?
Access to credit for women's enterprises
Amsterdam, January 1991

Agnes J. Angeles, Vice President, Planters Development Bank, Philippines

Jaya Arunachalam, Working Women's Forum, Madras, India

Nancy Barry, President, Women's World Banking, New York, USA

Lynn Bennett, PHRWD, World Bank, Washington D.C., USA

Maria E. Carvajal, Microenterprise Development Officer, Carvajal Foundation, Cali, Colombia

Guido Delgado, Managing Director, Northern Mindanao Development Bank, Cagayan de Oro, Philippines

Vera Gianotten, Programme Leader, Enterprise Development Programme, Royal Tropical Institute, Amsterdam, The Netherlands

John Grierson, Enterprise Development Programme, Royal Tropical Institute, Amsterdam, The Netherlands

S.K. Gupta, Director, Financial Systems Development, AT International, Washington, D.C., USA

Evelien Herfkens, Member of the Board of Directors, World Bank, Washington D.C., USA

Muzammel Huq, Director Training and Special Programmes, Grameen Bank, Dhaka, Bangladesh

Humaira Islam, Project Director, Women's Credit Programme, Dhaka, Bangladesh

Sigridur Kristmundsdottir, Board Member, ICEIDA, Reykjavik, Iceland

Robert J. Latowsky, Research Associate, State University of New York, Binghamton, New York, USA

Sheila Letshwiti, General Manager, Botswana Craft Company, Gaborone, Botswana

Cornelia Lohmar - Kuhnle, GITEC Consult Gmbh, Düsseldorf, Germany

Rose Njeri Mwaniki, Werep Ltd., Nairobi, Kenya

Mary E. Okelo, Director and Senior Advisor to the President, Women's World Banking, Nairobi, Kenya

Rosa P. Pinheiro, OMCV, Cape Verde, West Africa

Theobaldo Pinzas, Research and Credit Officer, Oxfam, Lima, Peru

Brian Pratt, Research Coordinator, Oxfam, Oxford, United Kingdom

Shashi Rajagopalan, Thrift and Credit Officer,
Samakya, Hyderabad, India

May Rihani, Associate Director (Women's
Programmes), Creative Associates International,
Washington D.C., USA

Aurora Riva, Director National Planning Office,
Lima, Peru

Frans van der Schuren, SUR, Fondo de
Pequenos Proyectos Productivos, Santiago, Chile

Hans Dieter Seibel, GTZ Credit Advisor to
PPHBK Bank Indonesia, Yogyakarta, Indonesia

Ingebjørg Støfring, Advisor, Unit for Women
and Environmental Issues, NORAD, Oslo,
Norway

Kristi-Anne Stølen, Centre For Development
and Environment, University of Oslo, Norway

Carle J. Walter, Executive Director, National
Development Foundation of Antigua and
Barbuda

Catherine van der Wees, Investment Officer,
Small Enterprise Department, Netherlands
Development Finance Company Ltd. (FMO),
The Hague, The Netherlands

Anne Zwahlen, Chief, Women in Development,
Swiss Development Cooperation, Bern,
Switzerland

Appendix 3: Symposium papers

Sharing poverty or creating wealth?
Access to credit for women's enterprises
Amsterdam, January 1991

Angeles, Agnes J.
Identifying the problem: an examination of the
financial and administrative aspects of restrict-
ed access to credit for women. 7 pp + annexes.

Arunachalam, Jaya
Sharing poverty or creating wealth? Access to
credit for women's enterprises. 23 pp. +
bibliography.

Barry, Nancy
State of the art on access to financial
mechanisms for women. 6 pp.

Carvajal, Maria
Support mechanisms of the microenterprise
development program carried out by the
Carvajal Foundation in Cali, Colombia. 3 pp.

Delgado, Guido Alfredo A.
Venture capital as an alternative form for
accessing funds for women. 18 pp. +
bibliography.

Gianotten, Vera
Sharing poverty or creating wealth. Access to
credit for women's enterprises, a general
outline. 10 pp.

Gupta, S.K.
On non-conventional forms of credit. 1 p.

Herfkens, Evelien
Opening address for symposium on 'Sharing
poverty or creating wealth? Access to credit for
women's enterprises'. 15 pp.

Huq, M.
Grameen Bank, a bank for the poor. 6 pp.

Kenya Rural Enterprise Programme
Programme description Kenya Rural Enterprise
Programme (K-REP). 6 pp.

Letshwiti, Sheila
The use of intermediaries to facilitate women's
access to credit. 5 pp.

Okelo, Mary
Do intermediaries result in increased access or
merely increased administration: the case of
Barclay's Banks and Women's World Banking
in Kenya. 12 pp.

Pratt, Brian
Pros and cons of the minimalistic and the
maximalistic approach. 3 pp.

Rajagapolan, S.
Women and development, some thoughts. 9 pp.

Riva, Aurora
Subsidized credit – pros and cons. The case of
Peru. 9 pp.

Seibel, H.D.
Microfinance for microenterprises: some
practical experiences of linkages between
formal and informal financial institutions in
Indonesia. 21 pp. + bibliography.

Stølen, Kristi Anne
The social and cultural context: women and development assistance. 14 pp. + bibliography.

Vanderschueren, Franz
Posibilidades y limites de la asistencia financiera a las microempresarias y dueñas de talleres productivos. 24 pp. + bibliography.

Wees, Catherine van der
The formal sector view on subsidised credit: lessons learned from the FMO. 8 pp. + bibliography.

Zapatos, Carolina C.
Identifying the problem: an examination of financial & administrative aspects in restricted access to credit. 10 pp.

Bibliography

Adams, D. W. (1986). 'Rural financial markets: The case against cheap credit'. *Ceres*, vol. 19, no. 1, pp. 15-18.

Adams, D. W. (1988). 'The conundrum of successful credit projects in floundering rural financial markets'. *Economic development and cultural change*, vol. 36, no. 2, pp. 355-367.

Adas, M. (1974). 'Immigrant Asians and the economic impact of European imperialism: The role of the South Indian Chettiars in British Burma'. *Journal of Asian studies*, vol. 33, no. 3, pp. 385-401.

Angeles, A. J. (1991). 'Identifying the problem: An examination of the financial and administrative aspects of restricted access to credit for women'. Paper presented at the symposium *Sharing poverty or creating wealth? Access to credit for women's enterprises*, Amsterdam, The Netherlands, 7th-9th January, 1991, 7 pp.

Arunachalam, J. (1991). 'Sharing poverty or creating wealth? Access to credit for women's enterprises'. Paper presented at the symposium *Sharing poverty or creating wealth? Access to credit for women's enterprises*. Amsterdam, The Netherlands, 7th-9th January, 1991, 23 pp.

Batley, R. and N. Devas (1988). 'The management of urban development: Current issues for aid donors'. *Habitat International*, vol. 12, no. 3, pp. 173-186.

Baud, I.S.A. (1989). *Forms of production and women's labour: Gender aspects of industrialization in India and Mexico.* (Ph.D. Thesis, Technical University Eindhoven, The Netherlands, 237 pp.)

Benería, L. and G. Sen (1981). 'Accumulation, reproduction, and women's role in economic development: Boserup revisted'. *Signs, Journal of Women in Culture and Society*, vol. 7, no. 2, pp. 279-298.

Bequele, A. and J. Boyden (1988). *Combating child labour.* Geneva, ILO, 226 pp.

Berger, M. (1989). 'Giving women credit: The strength and limitations of credit as a tool for alleviating poverty'. *World Development*, vol. 17, no. 7, pp. 1017-1030.

Berger, M. and M. Buvinic (eds.) (1989). *Women's ventures: Assistance to the informal sector in Latin America.* West Hartford, Kumarian Press, 266 pp.

Berik, G. (1987). 'Women carpet weavers in rural Turkey: Patterns of employment, earnings and status'. Geneva, International Labour Office, Women, work and development no. 15, 112 pp.

Bhattacharya, D. (1990). *Rural poverty alleviation through non-farm employment programmes.* Dhaka, Bangladesh Institute of Development Studies, 130 pp.

Boomgaard, J. J. (1989). 'AID. Microenterprise stock-taking: Synthesis report'. *AID Evaluation Special Study*, no. 65, Washington, USAID, 84 pp.

Bottomly, A. (1975). 'Interest rate determination in underdeveloped rural areas'. *American Journal of Agricultural Economics*, vol. 57, pp. 279-291.

Bouman, F. J. A. (1977). *Indigenous savings and credit societies in the Third World – Any message?* Report of a conference on Rural Finance Research, San Diego, California, July 28 - August 1, 43 pp.

Bouman, F. J. A. (1984). 'Informal savings and credit arrangements in developing countries: Observations from Sri Lanka'. In: D.L. Adams, D.H. Graham and J.D. von Pischke (eds.), *Undermining rural development with cheap credit*. Boulder, Westview Press, pp. 232-247.

Bouman, F. J. A. (1989). *Small, short and unsecured: Informal rural finance in India.* Delhi, Oxford University Press, 136 pp.

Bouman, F. J. A. (1990). 'Informal rural finance, an Aladdin's lamp of information'. *Sociologia Ruralis*, vol. 30, no. 2, pp. 155-173.

Bruce, J. (1989). 'Homes divided'. World Development, vol. 17, no. 7, pp. 979-991.

Brydon, L. and S. Chant (1989). *Women in the third world, gender issues in rural and urban areas.* Aldershot, Edward Elgar Press, 327 pp.

Buvinic, M. and M. Berger (1990). 'Sex differences in access to a small enterprise development fund in Peru'. *World Development*, vol. 18, no. 5, pp. 695-705.

Carr, M. (1990). 'Women in small-scale industries; Some lessons from Africa'. *Small Enterprise Development*, vol. 1, no. 1, pp. 47-51.

Carvajal, M. (1991). 'Support mechanisms of the microenterprise development program carried out by the Carvajal foundation in Cali, Colombia'. Paper presented at the symposium *Sharing poverty or creating wealth? Access to credit for women's enterprises*, Amsterdam, The Netherlands, 7th-9th January, 1991, 3 pp.

Chen, M. (1989). 'Women and entrepreneurship; new approaches from India'. In: A. Gosses, K. Molenaar, Q. Sluys and R. Tezler (eds.), *Small enterprises, new approaches*. The Hague, Ministry of Foreign Affairs, pp. 139-150.

Clark, M. H. (1984). 'Woman-headed households and poverty: Insights from Kenya'. *Signs: Journal of women in culture and society*, vol. 10, no. 21, pp. 338-354.

Cloud, K. (1985). 'Women's productivity in agricultural systems: Considerations for project design'. In: C. Overholt, M. Anderson, K. Cloud and J. Austin, *Gender roles in development: A case book.* West Hartford, Kumarian Press, pp. 17-56.

Commonwealth Expert Group on women and structural adjustment (1989). *Engendering adjustment for the 1990's.* Commonwealth Secretariat, London, 139 pp.

Deere, C.D. (1984). 'Rural women and agrarian reform in Peru, Chile and Cuba'. In: *Women on the move: Contemporary changes in family and society*, Paris, UNESCO, pp. 57-81.

DeLancey, V. (1978). 'Women at the Cameroon Development Corporation: How their money works'. *Rural Africana*, no. 2, pp. 9-33.

Delgado, G. A. A. (1991). 'Venture capital as an alternative form for accessing funds for women, the case of Northern Mindanao Development Bank, Philippines'. Paper presented at the symposium

Sharing poverty or creating wealth? Access to credit for women's enterprises, Amsterdam, The Netherlands, 7th-9th January, 1991, 18 pp.

Devereux, S. and H. Pares with J. Best (1987). 'A manual of credit & savings for the poor of developing countries'. Oxford, OXFAM, *Development Guidelines*, no. 1, 70 pp.

Dixon-Mueller, R. (1985). *Women's work in Third World agriculture, concepts and indicators.* Geneva, ILO, 151 pp.

Donald, G. (1976). *Credit for small farmers in developing countries.* Boulder, Westview Press, 275 pp.

Downing, J. (1991). 'Gender and the growth of microenterprises'. *Small Enterprise Development*, vol. 2, no. 1, pp. 4-13.

Drake, P.J. (1980). *Money, Finance and Development.* Oxford, Oxford University Press.

Du Marchie Sarvaas, E.C. (1989). 'Revolving Funds: een begrip?' Wageningen, Landbouw Universiteit, 69 pp. (Unpublished.)

Dulansey, M. and J. Austin (1985). 'Small-scale enterprise and women'. In: C. Overholt, M. Anderson, K. Cloud and J. Austin. *Gender roles in development: A case book.* West Hartford, Kumarian Press, pp. 79-131.

Elkan, W. (1973). *An Introduction to Development Economics*, Harmondsworth, Penguin, 155 pp.

Elson, D. (1989). 'How is structural adjustment affecting women?'. *Development Journal*, SID, no. 1, pp. 67-83.

Epstein, T. S. (1990). 'Female entrepreneurs and their multiple roles'. In: S. Vyakarnam (ed.), *When the harvest is in: Developing rural entrepreneurship.* London, Intermediate Technology Publications, pp. 254-265.

Floro, S.L. and P.A. Yotopoulos (1991). *Informal credit markets and the new institutional economics: The case of Philippine agriculture.* Boulder, Westview Press, 146 pp.

Gamser M. and F. Almond (1989). 'The role of technology in microenterprise development'. In: J. Levitsky (ed.), *Microenterprises in developing countries.* London, Intermediate Technology Publications, pp. 189-201.

Gianotten, V., Riofrío, G., Bueningen, C. van and C. van Kooten (1990). *Las mujeres del grupo destinatario: La mujer en programas de promoción urbana en el Peru.* Lima, Informe de evaluación DGIS-CEBEMO, 68 pp.

Grierson, J. P. and R.J. Latowsky (1992). 'Skills training for self-employment: Traditional apprenticeships and enterprise support networks'. (To be published in *Small Enterprise Development.*)

Grown, C. A. and J. Sebstad (1989). 'Introduction: Toward a wider perspective on women's employment'. *World Development*, vol. 17, no. 7, pp. 937-952.

Haan, H.C. (1990). 'Rural non-farm employment in Africa: Options for support interventions'. (Unpublished.)

Haan, H.C. (1991). 'Rural informal employment'. In: H.C. Haan (ed.) *Skills training for rural employment in the Philippines*. ILO, Manilla, pp. 13-24

Haggblade, S., Hazell, P. and J. Brown (1989). 'Farm-nonfarm linkages in rural Sub-Saharan Africa'. *World Development*, vol. 17, no. 8, pp. 1173-1201.

Hammam, S. (1989). *Informal savings and credit in West Africa*. Washington, National Savings and Loan League, Office of Housing and Urban Development, 67 pp.

Hancock, G. (1989). *Lords of Poverty: The freewheeling lifestyles, power, prestige and corruption of the multi-billion dollar aid business*. London, Macmillan, 234 pp.

Harper, M. (1989). 'Training and technical assistance for microenterprise'. In: J. Levitsky (ed.), *Microenterprises in developing countries*. London, Intermediate Technology Publications, pp. 177-188.

Harper, M. and W. Momm (1989). *Self-employment for disabled people: Experiences from Africa and Asia*. Geneva, ILO, 84 pp.

Harriss, B. (1987). 'Regional growth linkages from agriculture and resource flows in non-farm economy'. *Economic and Political Weekly*, vol. 22, no. 1 and 2, pp. 31-46.

Hogan, A.J. (1982). *The role of crop credit insurance in the agricultural credit system in developing economies*. Madison, University of Wisconsin, 217 pp.

Holt, S. L. and H. Ribe (1990). *Developing financial institutions for the poor: Reducing gender barriers*. Washington, World Bank, Policy, Research and External Affairs Division, 36 pp.

Howell, J. (ed.) (1980). *Borrowers & lenders, rural financial markets and institutions in developing countries*. London, Overseas Development Institute, 290 pp.

Huppi, M. and G. Feder (1990). 'The role of groups and credit cooperatives in rural lending'. *The World Bank Research Observer*, vol. 5, no. 2, pp. 187-204.

Huq, M. (1991). 'Grameen Bank: A bank for the poor'. Paper presented at the symposium *Sharing poverty or creating wealth? Access to credit for women's enterprises*, Amsterdam, The Netherlands 7th-9th January, 1991, 6 pp.

Hurley, D. (1990). 'Income generation schemes for the urban poor'. Oxford, Oxfam, *Development Guidelines*, no. 4, 136 pp.

Inter-American Development Bank (1988). *Working Paper* no. 4, 1988. Sectorial Policies Division, 26 pp.

Iqbal Z. and A. Mirakhor (1987). Islamic banking. International Monetary Fund, Washington, *Occasional Paper* no. 49, 62 pp.

Jackelen, H. R. (1989). 'Banking on the informal sector'. In: J. Levitsky (ed.), *Microenterprises in developing countries*. London, Intermediate Technology Publications, pp. 131-143.

Jong, M. de and N. Kleiterp (1991). 'Credit for small business and microenterprises in developing countries'. *Small Enterprise Development*, vol. 2, no. 4, pp. 21-30.

Kandiyoti, D. (1990). 'Women and rural development policies: The changing agenda'. *Development and Change*, vol. 21, pp. 5-22.

Kilby, P. and C. Liedholm (1986). 'The role of nonfarm activities in the rural economy'. Washington, USAID, *EEPA Discussion Paper* no. 7, 75 pp.

König, W. and M. Koch (1990). 'External financing of microenterprises in LDCs: Lessons from Colombia'. *Savings and Development*, vol. 14, no. 3, pp. 233-245.

Kratoska, P.H. (1975). 'The Chettiar and the yeoman: British cultural categories and rural indebtness in Malaya'. Singapore, Institute of Southeast Asian Studies, *Occasional Paper* no. 32, 20 pp.

Kropp, E., Marx, M., Pramos, B., Quinones, B., and H.D. Seibel (1989). *Linking self-help groups and banks in developing countries.* Bangkok, APRACA and GTZ, Eschborn, 145 pp.

Kuiper, M. (1988). 'Women and entrepreneurs in Africa, an exploration of factors influencing the involvement and performance of African women in small enterprise'. (Unpublished.)

Kuiper, K (1989). *Revolving funds.* The Hague, Development Cooperation Information Department, Netherlands Ministry of Foreign Affairs, 21 pp.

Levitsky, J. (1987). *World Bank experience in the financing of small enterprise.* The Hague, Institute of Social Studies. (Policy Workshop on Small Scale Industrialization.) 14 pp.

Levitsky, J. (1989). 'Summary report of conference'. In: J. Levitsky (ed.), *Microenterprises in developing countries, papers and proceedings of an international conference.* London, Intermediate Technology Publications.

Liedholm, C. (1990). 'The dynamics of small-scale industry in Africa and the role of policy'. The Hague, Institute of Social Studies, *Industrialization seminar paper* nr. 90-4/7, 50 pp.

Little, I., Mazumdar, D., and J. Page (1987). 'Small Manufacturing Enterprises: A comparative study of India and other economies'. New York, Oxford University Press, *World Bank Research Paper*, 362 pp.

Lyberaki, A. and I. Smyth (1990). 'Small is small: The role and functions of small-scale industries'. In: M.P. van Dijk and H. Secher Marcussen (eds.), *Industrialization in the third world: The need for alternative strategies.* Frank Cass, London, pp. 125-145.

Lycklama à Nijeholt, G. (1987). 'The fallacy of integration: The UN strategy of integrating women into development revisted'. *Netherlands Review of Development Studies*, vol. 1, pp. 57-71.

Mahadevan, R. (1978). 'Immigrant entrepreneurs in colonial Burma: An exploratory study of Nattukottai Chettiars of Tamil Nadu, 1880-1930'. *The Indian Economic and Social History Review*, vol. 15, no. 3, pp. 329-358.

Maloney, C. and A.B. Ahmed (1988). *Rural savings and credit in India.* Dhaka, University Press Limited, 242 pp.

Marion, P. (1990). Credit union achievements in developing countries. In: J. Bayley and E. Parnell (eds.), *Yearbook of cooperative enterprise 1990.* Oxford, Plunkett Foundation, 35-52 pp.

McKee, K. (1989). 'Microlevel strategies for supporting livelihoods, employment, and income generation of poor women in the Third World: The challenge of significance'. *World Development*, vol. 17, no. 7, pp. 993-1006.

Meilink, H. (1991). 'Structural adjustment and food security in Sub-Saharan Africa: Some indications'. Notes supporting the third evaluation of the DGIS/VPO programme. Leiden, Afrika Studie Centrum. (Unpublished.)

Meyer, R. L. (1989). 'Financial services for microenterprises: Programmes or markets?' In: J. Levitsky (ed.), Microenterprises in developing countries. London, Intermediate Technology Publications, pp. 121-131.

Meyer, R. L. and G. Nagarajan (1988). 'Financial services for small and microenterprises: A need for policy changes and innovation'. *Savings and Development*, vol. 12, no. 4, pp. 363-373.

Miller, L.F. (1977). *Agricultural Credit and Finance in Africa*. New York, Rockefeller Foundation, 115 pp.

Ministerie van Landbouw en Visserij (1988). *Krediet en spaarvormen op het platteland in de derde wereld*. Wageningen, Ministerie van Landbouw en Visserij, 33 pp.

Mobassar Husain, M. (1990). 'NGO experiences'. Paper presented at the seminar *Employment promotion & poverty alleviation in Rural Bangladesh*, Dhaka, ARPLA/ILO, 8-11 October, 1990.

Morss, E.E., Hatch, J.K., and D.R. Mickelwait (1976). *Strategies for Small Farmer Development: An empirical study of rural development projects in: The Gambia, Ghana, Kenya, Lesotho, Nigeria, Bolivia, Colombia, Mexico, Paraguay and Peru*. Boulder, Westview Press, 2 volumes, 444 pp.

Moser, C. O. N. (1989). 'Gender planning in the third world: Meeting practical and strategic gender needs'. *World Development*, vol. 17, no. 11, pp. 1799-1825.

NIO-vereniging (1989). *Krediet voor vrouwen, een speurtocht naar optimale krediet verlening voor vrouwen in ontwikkelingslanden*. Amsterdam, NIO-vereniging, 70 pp.

Noponen, H. (1990). 'Loans to the working poor: A longitudinal study of credit, gender, and the household economy'. New Brunswick (USA), Center for urban affairs, *Working Paper* no. 6, Rutgers University, 27 pp.

Okelo, M. (1991). 'Do intermediaries result in increased access or merely increased administration: The case of Barclay's Bank and Women's World Banking in Kenya'. Paper presented at the symposium *Sharing poverty or creating wealth? Access to credit for women's enterprises*. Amsterdam, The Netherlands, 7th-9th January, 1991, 12 pp.

Operations Review Unit (ORU) (1988). *Women entrepreneurs, development prospects for women entrepreneurs in small and micro scale industry*. The Hague, Ministry of Foreign Affairs, 83 pp.

Oppenoorth, H. (1990). *De un Programa de Emergencia hacia una alternativa de desarrollo: El caso de los fondos rotativos de papa-Anta-Cusco-Peru*. CADEP 'JMA', Cusco, Peru, 136 pp.

Overholt, C., Anderson, M., Cloud K. and J. Austin (eds.) (1985). *Gender roles in development: A case book*. West Hartford, Kumarian Press, 326 pp.

Page, J. M. (1979). 'Small enterprise in African development: A survey'. *Staff Working Paper* no. 363, World Bank, 53 pp.

Palmer, I. (1985). 'The impact of agrarian reform on women. Women's role and gender differences in development', *Monograph*, no. 6. West Hartford, Kumarian Press, 55 pp.

Perano, B., and H. Pössinger (1987). 'Ländliche Entwicklung in Chile. Kredit und Revolving Funds in der Kirchlichen Entwicklungsarbeit'. *Misereor Dialog* 4, Aachen, 175 pp.

Pischke, J.D. von, Heffernan, P. J. and D.W. Adams (1981). 'The political economy of specialized farm credit institutions in low-income countries'. Washington, *Staff Working Paper*, no. 446, World Bank, 99 pp.

Pischke, J.D. von, D.W. Adams and G. Donald (eds.) (1983). *Rural financial markets in developing countries: Their use and abuse.* Baltimore, John Hopkins University Press, 441 pp.

Popiel, P. A. (1990). 'Developing financial markets in Sub-Saharan Africa', *EDI Working Papers*, Washington, World Bank, Economic Development Institute.

B. Pratt, Savara, M. and F, Babiker Mahoud (1988). *The Evaluation of ACORD,* Port Sudan, Small Business Programme.

Pye, E. A. (ed.) (1988). *Artisans in economic development: Evidence from Asia.* Ottawa, International Development Research Center, 125 pp.

Rajagopalan, S. (1991). 'Women and employment, some thoughts'. Paper presented at the symposium *Sharing poverty or creating wealth? Access to credit for women's enterprises.* Amsterdam, The Netherlands, 7th-9th January, 1991, 9 pp.

Seibel, H. D. (1989). 'Finance with the poor, by the poor, for the poor: Financial technologies for the informal sector, with case studies from Indonesia'. *Social Strategies Forschungsberichte*, vol. 3, no. 2, pp. 3-45.

Seibel, H. D. (1991). 'Microfinance for microenterprises: Some practical experiences of linkages between formal and informal financial institutions in Indonesia'. Paper presented at the symposium *'Sharing poverty or creating wealth? Access to credit for women's enterprises,* Amsterdam, The Netherlands, 7th-9th January, 1991, 21 pp.

Slob, A. (1991). 'Vrouwen en krediet: mythen en feiten'. *Internationale Spektator*, vol. 14, no. 6, pp. 354-360.

Soto, H. de (1986). *El otro sendero, la revolución informal,* Lima, Ed. el Barranco

Staudt, K. (1987). 'Uncaptured or unmotivated? Women and the food crisis in Africa'. *Rural Sociology*, vol. 52, no. 1, pp. 37-55.

Steunpunt Eigen Werk (STEW) (1990). *Vrouwen bedrijven in Amsterdam: een faktor van betekenis.* Amsterdam, STEW, 48 pp.

Stølen, K. A. (1991). 'The social and cultural context: Women and development assistance'. Paper presented at the symposium *Sharing poverty or creating wealth? Access to credit for women's enterprises,* Amsterdam, The Netherlands, 7th-9th January, 1991, 14 pp.

Sundar, P. (1983). 'Credit for self-employment of women'. *Discussion Paper* 2, 75 pp. (Unpublished.)

Tovo, M. (1991). 'Microenterprise among village women in Tanzania'. *Small Enterprise Development*, vol. 2, no. 1 pp. 20-31.

UNDP, Government of the Netherlands, ILO, UNIDO (RSIE) (1988). *Development of rural small industrial enterprises, lessons from experience.* Vienna, 178 pp.

UNICEF (1987). *The invisible adjustment: Poor women and the economic crisis.* Santiago, Chile, Alfa Beta Impresores.

Union de Cooperativas Ejidales (UCE) (1988). *Crédito campesino.* Oaxaca, Mexico, 27 pp.

UN (1991). 'The world's women 1970-1990, Trends and statistics', *United Nations Social Statistics and Indicators Series*, K no. 8, New York, 120 pp.

Wai, U. Tun (1972). *Financial intermediation and national savings in developing countries.* New York, Praeger, 241 pp.

Wees, C. van der and H. Romijn (1987). *Entrepreneurship and small enterprise development for women in developing countries: An agenda of unanswered questions.* Geneva, ILO, Management Development Branch, 90 pp.

White, B. (1991). 'Studying women and rural non-farm sector development in West Java', *Project Working Paper Series*, no. B-12; ISS-PSP-IPB/PPLH. Institute of Social Studies and Bandung Research Project Office, 45 pp.

Whitehead, A. (1985). 'Effects of technological change on rural women: A review of analysis and concepts'. In: I. Ahmed (ed.) *Technology and rural women: Conceptual and empirical issues.* London, George Allen & Unwin for the ILO World Employment Programme, pp. 27-64.

World Bank (1974). 'Agricultural Credit'. *Rural Development Series*, Washington, 57 pp.

Yaron, J. (1991). *Successful rural financial institutions.* AGRAP, World Bank, 70 pp. (Draft.)

Young, K. (1988). 'Introduction: Reflections on meeting women's needs'. In: K. Young (ed.), *Women and economic development. Local, regional and national planning strategies.* Paris, UNESCO, pp. 1-30.

Zapatos, C. C. (1991). 'Identifying the problem: An examination of financial & administrative aspects in restricted access to credit'. Paper presented at the symposium *'Sharing poverty or creating wealth? Access to credit for women's enterprises'*, Amsterdam, The Netherlands, 7th-9th January, 1991, 10 pp.

Zineldin, M. (1990). *The economics of money and banking, a theoretical and empirical study of Islamic interest-free banking.* Stockholm University, Department of Business Administration, 276 pp.

0755